An Eastern View of Jesus Christ
Divine Discourses of Sathya Sai Baba

Translated by Lee Hewlett & K Nataraj
Forward by Sir George Trevelyan Bt. M.A.

Sai Publications

DEDICATION

*This book is
dedicated to
Bhagavan
Sathya Sai Baba
and Jesus Christ
without whom nothing
would have
been possible.*

*Bhagavan is a title
which means Bringer
of True Enlightment*

ACKNOWLEDGEMENTS

The Publishers acknowledge with humility and love Sai Baba's permission to publish these Divine Discourses in the West for the first time. This is an American translation.

Printed by: Parish Partners, 7 Elsynge Road, SW18 2HW.

PREFACE

by Sir George Trevelyan Bt M.A.

Many thousands of people throng to meet the Indian Man of God
Bhagavan Sathya Sai Baba. It appears that he is much more than
another great guru or teacher. He is an examplar of what is now
happening in the world, the incarnation of Divinity within the human
being. In him is manifested the great hope for our tormented world —
that God can enter human life with the transforming power of love.

The doctrine of the Avatar implies that when human need is desperate
and the cry for help is sent up, the Saviour appears. To quote from the
Bhagavad Gita:-

*"Whenever there is a withering of the law and an uprising of
lawlessness on all sides, then I manifest Myself. For the salvation
of the righteous and the destruction of such as do evil, for the
firm establishing of the law, I come to birth age after age."*

This coming of the power of Universal Love which can light up in every
heart, is indeed the impulse that can lead us into a new Age of Peace
and harmony. All the great religions expect such a visitation. We, as
Christians, wait for the Second Coming of Christ, the universal and
exalted Being of Light who manifested in Jesus 2000 years ago. The
hope of the Coming One is the note and meaning of our age. As
Teilhard de Chardin wrote, it is "the wild hope that our earth is to be
recast." All the signs and communications indicate that the Divine
Power of redemptive Love is indeed being flooded into Earth now, and
of course it will enter through the attuned hearts of individual men and
women. The violence and brutality of our time can be seen as the
desperate effort of the powers of darkness to capture the human soul
and intellect before it is too late, for as the Apocalyptic passage decrees
(Revelation 12): the Beast is cast down to earth by the Archangel
Michael, "having great wrath because he knoweth that he hath but a
short time."

Bhagavan Sathya Sai Baba is recognised and experienced by so many as
a God-Man, an Avatar of Love. Love is the Light of the Spiritual Sun
and shines on all men. Furthermore, the great discovery and realisation
of our age is that all life is one great intricate web, that the Universe is
not empty space but a vast and living whole, an ocean of divine creative
Mind and Intelligence, which has poured itself out into the infinite
forms of nature. Advanced scientific thinking now arrives at the
knowledge of Oneness which the mystics have always experienced. The
New Religion will perforce be universal. There can be nothing sectarian
about Truth. All the great prophets in every religion have stated
mankind's Golden Rules in almost the same words:-

"Do unto others as you would have them do unto you."

Sai Baba in his teaching and in his entire Being is a channel for the Universal Love which will unite all men. He gives us now this beautiful book about Jesus and the Christ impulse, written in a style which all can grasp with ease, but which touches profound depths. I quote one passage which summarizes all he is saying:-

> *There are not countless religions.*
> *There is only one religion —*
> *the religion of Divine Love.*
> *There is only one race —*
> *the race of mankind.*
> *There is only one language —*
> *the language of Divine Love in your heart.*
> *There is only one God.*
> *He is present everywhere.*

It is of paramount importance that we bridge the gap between East and West. Many who are in quest of spiritual understanding have gone to India to find their guru who can teach the profound wisdom of the Orient. Yet we in the West also have our own mystery tradition for initiation into higher knowledge, which stems from the Mystery Temples of antiquity. It appears that Jesus the Christ in a profound sense fulfilled the ancient mysteries and brought us into the world an impulse which could unite and transform mankind. The Second Coming is primarily an inner event, a transformation of the heart centre through unflooding of a love which reveals that every soul is an eternal and imperishable droplet of Divinity. In this knowledge East meets West and science now unites with mysticism.

It is a joy that Sai Baba of India gives us this book about Jesus. In the greatness of his being he knows tha the redemption of our embattled world will come through the outpouring of the Waters of the Spirit, for which he is so wonderful a channel. This inflow characterizes the dawn of the Aquarian Age. This book is therefore about the way of attuning so that each soul can become a chalice for the Divine Light. Every man is the embodiment of God. The kernel of every soul is Divine and cannot know death, whatever happens to the bodily sheath. Here is a message of hope for all. Christ is coming and is present and as God is already manifesting in the great Masters of whom Satya Sai Baba is surely one. May we give thanks and praise.

George Trevelyan

Sir George Trevalyan Bt M.A.

CONTENTS

Published and produced by SAI PUBLICATIONS
Devereux House, 50 Longley Road
London S.W.17
ISBN 0 907785 02 6

PRELUDE

"King Herod ordered a census.
Each person had to return to
his native village to be counted.
Mary and Joseph made their way
along the road toward Bethlehem.
Mary was with child.
The pains began.
They knew no one nearby,
so they took refuge in a cow shed.
Joseph made a space between two cows.
It was midnight.
He went out to find
a woman who could help.
Then he heard a baby cry.
Christ was born.
A huge aura of splendor
filled the sky with light.
This was a sign
that He had overcome
the darkness of evil
and ignorance.
The light of Love
had come into the world.
It was the dawn of
the era of Divine Guidance.
To celebrate Jesus's Christ Birthday,
we should follow
the simple practical lessons
He gave us
for our spiritual advancement.
Follow His brave example.
Experience God as He did."

Sai Baba

THE CROSS

1. At dusk one evening
   in early March 1973,
   Sai Baba 1
   walked along
   a dry river bed
   with a Western pilgrim
   named Dr. Hislop

2. As He passed a small bush
   He pulled off two twigs,
   placed them one over the other
   and held them up.
   "What is this?", He said.
   Doctor Hislop replied,
   "It reminds me
   of the Christian Cross." 2

3. Sai folded His hand
   over the twigs and blew
   into His hand three times.
   When He opened His hand
   it held a small crucifix.

4. As He gave the crucifix
   to Dr. Hislop, He said,
   "This shows Christ 3
   as He really was
   at the time when
   He left His body.
   No writer or artist
   has imagined Him
   this way before.
   The wood
   is wood from the orignal cross
   on which Jesus 2 was crucified.
   To find that piece of wood
   took a little work."

5. Dr. Hislop asked about
   the hole at the top of the cross
   above Jesus' head.
   Sai explained that
   when the cross was used,
   it was hung
   from a wooden upright
   and supported by a large nail
   which extended through the hole.

6. Imagine the significance
   of an actual likeness of Jesus
   in the world today.

THE LIFE OF SAI BABA

1. In the early morning
   of November 23rd. 1926,
   there was jubilation
   in the corner house
   on the main road,
   in the remote Indian village
   of Puttaparti.

2. Pedda Venkapa Raju,
   a landowner
   had a son.
   They named the boy
   Sathya 1 Narayana Raju.

3. From the beginning
   there was something unusual
   about little Sathya.
   As He grew older
   He began to exhibit
   a high degree of will power.
   He would leave home
   whenever meat was served.
   He refused His own food
   rather than see a beggar
   go hungry.
   He never seemed
   to be affected by hunger,
   and He took odd jobs
   after school
   so that He would not
   have to accept money
   from His father.

4. The local boys
   found in Him a great friend.
   He was always able
   to provide for their needs
   in some mysterious way.
   He produced
   school supplies,
   sweets,
   sugar lumps
   and any kind of fruit
   they could imagine
   or ask for.
   He also helped them
   find lost items,
   gave them counsel when needed
   and encouraged them
   to do well
   in their school work.

5. In some strange way
    He was always
    able to answer
    any question
    that was put to Him.
    His school examination papers
    were flawless.
    He was the best
    boy scout in the troop
    and excelled
    in every athletic event.

6. He helped the boys to
    stage spiritual dramas,
    led daily religious services
    before school
    and led campaigns
    against cruelty to animals.

    His teachers found Him
    amazingly truthful
    and His behavior
    made Him a delight
    to have in class.

7. His parents hoped
    He would have an important career.
    On April 8th. 1940
    during His 14th, Year,
    He inexplicably fell into
    a trance-like state.
    As He recovered consciousness,
    He exhibited a knowledge
    of the Scriptures
    far beyond any local person's.

8. One morning
    in October of that same year
    He announced,
    "The illusion is over.
    Realize I am Sai Baba, 1
    the Divine Father of humanity:
    My followers are waiting;
    My mission must begin."
    From that day
    He made His home in
    a nearby temple area
    and became known
    as Sathya Sai Baba.

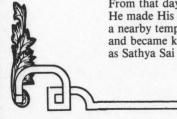

9. He performed many miracles.
    Small amounts of food
    became enough to feed thousands.
    The ill and deformed
    became well and whole.
    To increase the faith of His followers,
    valuable religious objects
    appeared from nowhere.
    People,
    who did not know Him,
    had visions of Him
    and came to see
    who He was.
    He seemed to know
    the past,
    present
    and future
    of everyone.
    He knew
    what was happening
    everywhere in the world.
    Sai Baba 1 was often seen
    in two or more places at once.
    "Dead" men awoke
    and lived out their lives.
    Doubters became spiritually inspired
    and gained faith in God.

10. After a time
    He defined his earthly mission.
    "I have come
    to revive the ancient wisdom
    contained in the Scriptures
    of every religion.
    Ignorance and misinterpretation
    must be destroyed.
    True spirituality
    must be understood
    and practised by humanity.
    The four pillars
    of spiritual life
    must be re-established.
    Timeless Truth,
    Infinite Peace
    and Divine Love
    must become
    a part of every life.
    Each person
    must live in harmony with
    the Divine Laws
    which govern life.

11. Peace and unity
must be restored
in the family,
the school,
the community,
the city,
the state
and the nations on Earth.
Schools must be established.
The just means of earning a living
must be taught.
The means of living
a virtuous life
and experiencing God's Grace
must be learned.

12. The human race
must be saved from destruction.
The methods of earning
both physical and spiritual comfort
must be practised.

13. I need no publicity.
I have no need or interest
in money or valuables.
Your love,
faith and devotion to God
are the gifts
which please me.
Let my miracles
remove your doubts.
Gain courage.
Drive out evil.
Lead a virtuous life.
Realize God.''

14. Avatars 1 come
from Age to Age
for the destruction of evil
and the salvation of the good.
Divine Harmony
will be restored on Earth.

15. Until the thirty second year
of His life,
miracles were emphasised.
From the age of thirty two
to the age of forty eight,
teachings were recorded.
"In the period between forty eight
and sixty four,

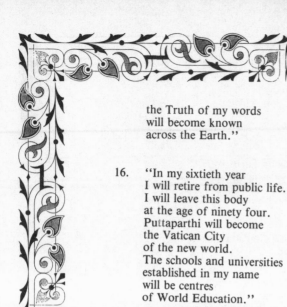

the Truth of my words
will become known
across the Earth."

16. "In my sixtieth year
I will retire from public life.
I will leave this body
at the age of ninety four.
Puttaparthi will become
the Vatican City
of the new world.
The schools and universities
established in my name
will be centres
of World Education."

17. "The Will of God
cannot be stopped.
The events God ordains
must take place,
The joyful Golden Age
will recur."

Follow
Jesus

"If anyone serves me,
He must follow me."

Jn. 12:26

"When we live and practise
Jesus' teachings
we are true Christians
— not before."

Sai
Christmas 1979:186

FOLLOW JESUS

1. "If anyone serves me,
    he must follow me." *John 12:26*
    When we live and practice
    Jesus' teachings
    we are true Christians —
    not before.

2. "Awaken, O sleeper,
    arise from the dead ...
    Be careful to follow
    the ways of truth
    not untruth.
    Walk as wise men.
    Leave ignorance behind.
    Make the most of your time
    because these are treacherous days".
    Ephesians 5:14-16

3. There is a reason
    that you are alive.
    The purpose of being human
    is to experience Unity
    with God.
    Regardless of your past
    or present conditions
    you can move
    through the stages
    Jesus 1 showed us
    during His life.

4. Rise above sorrow, pain
    and short-lived excitement.
    Realize the source
    of all problems
    and their simple resolution.
    Resolve the conflicts
    in your life.
    Live happily
    by the Golden Rule of life.
    Develop piercing insight,
    calm resolve
    and sound judgement.

    Find out what God
    wants you to do.
    Remold your character
    along godly lines.
    Know what is best
    and gain courage enough
    to do it.

5. Practice the spiritual disciplines
    necessary to take you
    along the path
    Jesus ı trod.
    Hear the Lord's name
    resounding in your heart.
    See Jesus
    ever with you.
    Become one
    with the Everlasting Light.
    Know God as your inner Self
    as Jesus did.

6. Serve yourself,
    humanity and God.
    God is Love.
    Divine Love
    is a positive force
    which cannot cause harm.
    Know the eternal,
    spiritual delight
    of God's Love.
    Taste the divine nectar
    of eternal peace.
    Who or what is God?

7. Some may deny
    the existence
    or importance of God.
    But the day will come
    When they have to give up
    their ignorant ways
    and pray for His compassion.
    Almost everyone has heard
    "God is everywhere.
    He knows everything.
    He is the all powerful
    Father of Humanity,
    who created everything in the universe
    including this Earth,
    you
    and the body you live in".
    We are also told
    that He is compassionate,
    the essence of Divine Love
    and the nature of Truth.
    Few realize
    Jesus' ı most important
    message to mankind.
    "God
    is your own basic nature —
    your true self."

What is Truth?
How can I find it?

8. There is only one Truth.
It is one of God's qualities.
To truly find
and understand Truth,
you will have to find
and experience God.
Until you experience something
you can only guess at
what it is.
What is truly
helpful to mankind?

9. In order to help mankind
we must understand
what mankind is
and what the purpose
of being human is.
By definition
the spiritual aspect of man
is a living Soul,
which inhabits a physical body.
Biologically man is called

Homo **sapiens sapiens.**
Here the word **Homo**
refers to the human body.
Sapiens means "wise".
Sapiens is used twice
because man is capable
of understanding
both the physical
and the spiritual.
He can know God.

What is the purpose
of being human?

10. God, the loving creator
of all things,
has given each of us
a human body
so that we may use it
to enrich our Souls
and serve Him on Earth
and thus glorify Him
by becoming one with Him
as Jesus 1 did.
What is a Soul?

11. A soul is
a living entity
which considers itself
in some way separate
from God.

How can we enrich our Souls?

12. God's wish
for each soul
is that it grows beyond
ideas of separation
and become fully aware
of its Unity
with the Almighty.

What does God
want me to do?

13. Part of the mission
of the Soul,
in its gradual development
toward God Realization,
is to do as Jesus 1 did
and be a living example
of God's unselfish Love.
This is the ideal way
to serve humanity,
by demonstrating
that one can achieve Divinity
while living on Earth
as a human.

How does my example help others?

Your quiet success
will show others
that peace, harmony,
Divine Love
and contentment
are possible
and worth achieving.
Your calmness,
composure,
humility,
purity, virtue,
courage and conviction
will encourage others
to follow Jesus.
Your mission is a great
responsibility:
You must teach mankind
by your every action.

Such is the purpose of life,
words alone are not enough.

Can Unity with God be achieved?

14.   Yes, it can be done.
This promise is made
by every religion.

Jesus ₁ gave His life
to show us the way.
There is no question
of it not being possible.

How can I become
a good example
for others?

15.   You must discover for yourself
which stage of spiritual development
you fit into;
then become determined
to progress
from class to class
in the school of life.
Take one step
at a time.
If you perform your duty
as thoroughly as possible,
you are bound
to win God's Grace
and move along
the road Jesus ₁ travelled,
so that we all might follow.

What exactly is God's Grace?

16.   Grace is "the gift from God" *Eph.2:8*
Grace is given in five ways:
First, in times of need,
God gives protection
with Divine Law.
Second, God gives
the divine strength necessary
to grow beyond ego
and narrow self-interest.
Third, God's Love gives
divine insight
and the wisdom to do what is right.
Such gifts allow one to be unaffected by
the ups and downs of life.

Fourth, God gives
so much Love
that one sees all
as one love-formed
harmonious creation
and feels the joy
of great Love for all.
Fifth, God gives the gift
of allowing the Soul
to merge into
His infinite, formless state.

Who can win God's Grace?

17. Any Soul may win Grace.
Why does not God's Grace
remove all suffering?

Every act a person does
creates a reaction.
You reap
whatever you have sown.
"He who sows sparingly,
will also reap sparingly." *2 Cor. 9:06*
How can God give
full time payment
for part-time devotion?

How may I win Grace?

18. At present you depend upon
your body for motivation.
You must end body-motivation.
Become God-motivated.
Realize that you
are not the body or ego.
Do not spend time
in unsacred ways.
Look to God.
Promote the best thoughts,
Words and deeds.
Desire God's Love.
Fill your mind and life
With Divine Love.

Let everything you do
be in accordance with
Divine Law.
Live Divine Law.
Moving towards Divinity
takes time
and effort on your part,
but Divine Law
will protect you

as the mother
protects her child.
God will give you
wisdom, love and Grace
according to your merit.
Keep this in mind always.

What are the levels of life
which must be passed through?

19. There are three levels of consciousness
which ascend from
a state of extreme ignorance
to a state of all-embracing
divine wisdom.

Please tell me more
about each level.

20. In the lowest state
a person has
little or no idea of God
or of his own true nature.
He is likely to feel
very heavy,
be very inactive
and self-centred.
He may be physically
or mentally ill.

21. The second phase
typifies life in
the ever-changing physical world.
In this stage
people divide their time
between actively pursuing worldly goods
and resting.

22. The third phase of awareness
is referred to by Jesus 1
as the "Kingdom of God"
or the "Kingdom of Heaven".
This level is far beyond
the reach of the senses.
One is in constant harmony
With God's unending Glory
and knows the everlasting life
of His divine nature.

How may I know
which level of spiritual awareness
I fit into?

23 Carefully and honestly
    examine your motives
    for seeking God.
    Take great care
    that your reason
    for turning to God
    is as noble as possible.

    Why do people turn to God?

24. Some people feel worn out
    by chronic illness;
    When God relieves their sickness,
    they forget Him
    until calamity strikes again.
    Others worry about
    their struggle for power,
    position, fame and wealth;
    To ensure success
    they turn to God
    for a holy guarantee.
    But once the hands are filled,
    They forget the Giver
    and bask
    in their short-lived
    material gains and pleasures.

    May you be
    in the third category.

    A person in this fortunate group
    is yearning continually
    for the comfort of God's Love.
    He craves to be
    one with the Father of All.
    He knows that
    the appropriate health
    and prosperity
    will be provided
    for his journey.

    What care does God
    give those who love Him?

25. God frees them
    from distractions,
    offers them Scriptures
    and books that enlighten,
    leads them into
    the right company
    and gives them spiritual teachers
    to help them live
    according to the Divine Laws
    of the spiritual life they deserve.

21

Their intelligence becomes sharper.
When the gates to God's Kingdom
swing open
they may take the opportunity
to accept the warm
and all-comforting
embrace of the Lord
for evermore.

Is it possible to become
One with God
as Jesus 1 did?

26.   Everyone who seeks God
must pass through the same stages
Jesus went through.
His divine campaign
showed all
that the death blows dealt
by the powers of darkness
could be overcome
by quiet discipline
and God's Love.

How should I begin
to follow Jesus?

27.   When we begin
our spritual practice,
character reform
and life of service to others,
we enter God's company
as a novice
who must remain watchful
lest he disobeys a commandment
and earns disfavor.
One must develop
the qualities of
absolute loyalty
and sincerity.
One must respect
God's every commandment,
serve Him faithfully
and surrender
to Divine Will,
without the slightest
reservation.
As one progresses,
he is given
the position of a trusted servant
with some small duties to perform.

28. This closeness to Divinity
    allows him to develop divine qualities
    and grow in spirituality.

    Gradually others begin
    to see him as an extension
    of the Lord's Hand
    and he earns the privilege
    of being recognized
    as a member
    of God's Holy Family.

29. When this third state matures,
    the separate self becomes
    lost in the Ultimate Self.
    God alone remains.
    All is One.
    Jesus 1 said,
    "I and My Father are One." 2
    You
    and your Heavenly Father
    will one day
    become One.

    How can I experience God
    as my own basic nature?

30. Take Jesus as your guide,
    Follow His example,
    Pass through the same stages of growth
    in awareness
    He passed through.
    Do spiritual practice.

    What is spiritual practice?

    Jesus progressed
    through several methods
    of spiritual practice
    in His life.
    To find correct methods of
    spiritual practice;
    each person must
    follow Jesus' example.

    What are the methods
    of spiritual practice
    Jesus followed?

    Jesus progressed from
    spiritual study
    to a concentrated
    search for God
    in the physical world.

Then He moved on to
inner visualization
and contemplation of God.

His final practice
was meditation on God
and union with God.

Are these methods of spiritual practice
described in the Bible?

31.   Regarding scriptural studies
Jesus said,
"If you love Me,
you will keep my commandments."
and
"Man shall live by
every word of God."
The physical method
of concentrating on God
is described
in Matthew and Romans:
"Whatever you ask for
in prayer
you shall receive ..."
and
"Whoever calls upon
the name of the Lord
shall be saved."
Spiritual visualization
of the Divine Form
is summarised
in the Book of John:
"I am the way ..."
"I am the door;
if anyone enters by me,
he will be saved ..."
The appropriate
subject of meditation
for merger
is given as follows:
"I am the Light of the World;
he who follows Me ...
will have the Light of Life."
"God is Light ..."

32   Therefore you follow
Jesus' 1 path
for the salvation of the Soul
by these practices:
you must live in Love,
study the Scriptures,
live by Divine Law,

pray to God,
call on Jesus constantly,
see His form in all,
feel Him always near,
and become One
with the Everlasting Light
which is God's essence.

How should the Scriptures
be studied?

33. We each owe Jesus
and the disciples
a great debt
for their gifts to mankind.
We must in all humility
bow our heads
over the Holy Scriptures
which would not exist
if Jesus 1 and the disciples
had not served God
on Earth.
While our heads are bowed,
we should read
with reverent concentration
and do our best
to understand the message
that Jesus is giving us.

34 The act of reading
is not enough
to purify the heart.
We must contemplate upon
the Scriptural passages
until we know
that we can practice them
in our daily lives.
If we truly love Jesus,1
we will devote the time necessary
to understanding the full import
of Biblical passages
and discuss them with others
who have had spiritual experiences.

35. Some people
may claim superior knowledge,
but in fact
be seeking for attention,
publicity
or financial gain.
Let these go their own ways.

36. It is wise
to form a spiritual study circle
with others who are honestly seeking
the spiritual life.
Exchange truths,
discuss virtues,
and listen to the glories of the Lord.
In a world
so full of people
who find time for gossip,
you can find time
to study Divinity.

37. Avoid bad company,
keep your heart ready
to absorb the Love of God.
Only Love
can take you to God.
A few uplifting lines
from the Scriptures
will resound in your heart.
Remember these
when you kneel
or sit to pray.
You will become calm
and the agitations
and entanglements of the world
will fade into the background.

What is prayer?
What is the purpose of prayers?

38. Prayer
is the breath of religion;
its purpose
is to bring man and God
together.
Prayer involves
asking the Lord
for whatever you desire.
You must always be careful
about your thoughts,
your unspoken prayers,
because God,
who is the ruler of all destiny,
will give you
what you ask for
if you ask sincerely.
But take great care.
Only ask Him for that
which is truly beneficial.

"Whatever you ask for
in prayer
you shall receive ..."*Matt 21:22*
Prayer for wealth
may eventually
make you rich,
but how many millionaires
find true happiness?

For what should we pray?

39. Forgiveness,
Eternal Life,
God's Love,
a vision of Jesus 1
the ability
to know what is right
and the courage
to follow the path of righteousness.

How should I pray?

40. Truly
your life should be
a constant prayer
for the salvation of the Soul.
To perfect this
even the most advanced souls
retire to a quiet place to pray
so they will not be disturbed.

41. It is best
to set aside
one place
as a sanctuary
for your daily prayers.
Do not pray
or meditate
in contact with bare earth.
Your precious energies
will be absorbed
or distrubed
by the Earth's pull.
Use a wooden platform
or ground cloth.
Go there twice a day.
The best time
is in the early morning
before the world awakens
and draws your attention.
An evening prayer period just
before you retire for the night
will also prove to be
of great value.

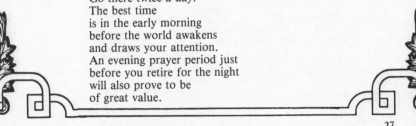

What is a good praying posture?

42. Sit in a comfortable,
relaxed position
with your back and neck
as straight as possible,
either in a chair
or on the floor.
The best practice is
to have a special ground cloth
used solely
for this purpose.
Either kneeling, or sitting on a cushion
with your legs crossed
is a good position for prayer,

so long as you are not
distracted by your body.
Shifting here and there,
due to a restless mind,
can make your worship
as hectic as
your daily life may be.
If you are travelling,
simply focussing your attention
on your prayer room
and prayers
at the appropriate times
will lift your spirits.

Should I have an altar?

43. Your heart
is the true altar:
keep your worldly altar simple.
Use a picture of Jesus, 1
a candle
and some fragrant incense.

Once I'm alone with God
what should I do?

44. If you
have begun
prayer immediately
after waking
as your first activity,
begin
immediately to concentrate
on the Lord's name.

If you have allowed
some other activity
to take first place
or it is your evening
prayer
you must relax.
Leave tension behind.
Turn your attention
fully to God.
Do so systematically.
Tighten each muscle,
and relax it.
Tighten and relax
your head muscles
one by one,
tighten and relax
the neck muscles,
shoulder muscles,
arms and hands;
then the back
and chest.

Next tighten and relax
the lower back,
legs and feet.
After relaxation of all the muscles,
you must relax the mind.

How can I relax the mind?

45. Take three, long, slow,
deep breaths. Repeat this
until the mind is calm.
Think of some Bible passages
or some stories of the Lord.
Then, when your mind is calm,
begin your morning prayer.
"Dear Lord,
You awaken me
and I am born
into a new day.
Make me speak
soft, sweet words,
and behave calmly
and compassionately towards all.
May I do good deeds
which bring happiness to all.
May I be an ideal example
as Jesus i was.
May I serve You well this day."

When should I begin morning prayers?

46.   Rise for prayer
at the same time each morning,
preferably
between 3 and 6 a.m.
Gradually
you will become fully adjusted
to your routine
and the touch of God
will awaken you daily.
At first you will pray
for only 10-15 minutes.
Then
as you feel the
elevating joy of peace,
the length of your prayer period
will gradually increase.

What do I do
for fifteen minutes?

47.   Jesus' [1] life was His message.
Follow the path He took;
Jesus began life
as God's Messenger;[2]

He became the Christed
Son of God; [3]
Finally He fulfilled His destiny
by becoming One with God. [4]
To progress through
the three levels of awareness
He passed through,
there are three divine disciplines
which you must perfect;
concentration on the Holy Name,
contemplation of the Divine Form
and meditation on God as Light.
The Name, the Form and Light are
the three keys
to spiritual awakening,
spiritual perfection
and spiritual immortality.
His Name, His Form, His Light.

How should I concentrate
on His Name?

48.   Jesus said, "Whoever calls upon
the name of the Lord
shall be saved." *Romans 10;13*

There is a simple way
to do this:
repeat Jesus' name.
"Jesus, Jesus, Jesus, Jesus ...,
Je's su, Je' su, Je'su ...,
or Ie'su, Ie'su, Ie'su."
You may repeat it
twenty to sixty times a minute
— three hundred, to
one hundred times
at a sitting.
If even one
of those times you say it
with full sincerity
that is an achievement.
By such prayer, the sins of the past
will gradually melt away.

Is it alright to use a rosary?

49.   A rosary
or prayer beads
will help your concentration.
Move one bead
with your right forefinger
each time you
say the Lord's name

May I use a longer prayer?

50.   In the beginning,
if you feel the need
for a longer prayer,
repeat, "Jesus Christ ı
please have mercy
on my Soul."
If a slightly different prayer
comes into your heart,
don't be afraid to use it.
God
will not mislead you,
but beware of
changing the prayer
once you settle on it.

How should I
end my prayer sessions?

51.   At the end of your prayers
do not jump up suddenly.
Move your knees gently.
Massage them a little
if necessary.

Recall the peace
Jesus 1 has given you.
Gently sing
three or more
slow amen's.
Get up slowly.
Then either return to your rest
or begin your day's work.

How should I end the evening prayers?

52. If it is
your evening prayer session,
entrust your Soul
to God
for the night.
Quickly examine
the events of your day.
See if your words
or actions
have caused pain
or displeasure to anyone.
Then pray, "Father,
as I fall into
your comforting arms,
please forgive me
for any weakness.
Give me the strength
of your Love."
Then resume calling on Jesus 1
until sleep comes.

Should I repeat
Jesus' name aloud
when I am alone?

53. During the early periods
of your prayers
you may need
to speak aloud
or in a whisper.
After a time
silent mouth movements
will be enough.
Finally,
you will hear
your inner voice
calling "Je'su, Je'su ..."
throughout the day.
This repetition of the Holy Name
will greatly increase
your devotion
and bring you divine peace.

How long will it take me
to progress through each stage
of awareness?

54.   Each person
has to move forward
from where he already happens to be
at his own pace,
motivated by his own inner urge,
along the path
God will reveal to him.
Only God
knows when you
will burst forth
into Divine Glory.

55.   Jesus 1 spent more than
seventeen years in prayer,
meditation
and service to mankind
before He announced
"I and My Father are One" 2
The growth of the Soul
is not a short term development.
Follow the same procedure every day:
Do not change the time,
duration,
method,
or position.
Distractions and disturbances
will be easily overcome.

How may I contemplate the form of Jesus?

56.   Jesus said, "I am the way ...
"I am the door;
if anyone enters by me,
he will be saved ... "
Chose a picture of Jesus 1
that inspires your heart.
Keep it before you
above your prayer altar.
Keep a picture of Jesus
where you work.
Carry one with you
wherever you go.

57.   When you find yourself

calling Jesus' name
almost automatically
from the moment you awaken
until you lose consciousness
at night,

you are ready
to start contemplating
the form of Jesus 1
shown in your picture of Him.

58.   As you repeat the name
in the morning prayer period,
begin to picture in your mind's eye
the form you love so well.
Start with His hair.
Draw each lock of hair separately.
Then fill in
His facial features
one by one.
You may do this
with your eyes open
or closed,
but be sure
not to stop calling
His Divine Name
while you are visualizing His form.

59.   Do this throughout the day
whenever you have a few minutes.
Always use the same picture.
Don't use Jesus the shepherd
in the morning,
Jesus as a twelve year old
in the temple
at noon,
and the infant Jesus
at night.

Remain with
whichever form you choose.
Don't change it.
Let it settle permantly in
your heart.

60.   When your thoughts wander
from the form of Jesus 1
focus on the name of Jesus.
If they wonder from the name
continue creating the form.
If the mind wanders a hundred times
bring it back a hundred times.
As the form stabilises,
you will see Jesus
more and more
as the living being
He really is.

You will see Him
and feel the warmth
of His closeness
and loving guidance,
no matter what happens
throughout the day.

How may I meditate on God as light?

61. Meditation on the Everlasting Light:
     Christ 1 said,
     "I am the Light ...,
     he who follows Me ...
     will have the Light of Life."
     "God is Light ..."

     When you see Jesus
     as your truest friend
     and call on Him always
     to keep your heart
     filled with joy,
     you are ready
     to begin meditation
     on the Everlasting Light.
     Remember that Scriptures says,
     "Awaken, O sleeper, and arise
     from the dead,
     and Christ shall give you Light."

62. Light a candle for Jesus 1
     at the beginning of your prayers.

     As you visualise Jesus
     and repeat His name,
     look at the candle
     then close your eyes.

     Visualise Jesus in the light,
     with light spreading from Him
     in all directions.
     Take the light
     into your body
     through the space between your eyebrows.
     Let the Light of Jesus
     move into your heart.
     Let your heart bloom
     as a flower of Light,
     opening one petal at the time.
     Gradually
     let the Light from Jesus 1
     grow bigger,
     wider,
     and brighter.

63. When it penetrates your mouth
any potential for falsehood,
slander and bragging
will vanish.
When it reaches the ears,
all thirst for scandal
will disappear.
When it includes the arms and legs,
they will lose their tendency
to engage in useless
or corrupt activities.
All dark desires
will be destroyed
by the brilliant
Light of Wisdom.
All vicious
or disturbing thoughts
will disappear.
Fill your entire body with Light.

64. As it grows brighter
and brighter,
let it shine all around you
and enfold you in Love.
Expand it
to include your family,
your loved ones,
your friends
and neighbours.
Surround strangers,
rivals and enemies
in the Light of Love.
Fill the whole world with Light.
Lighten all mankind.
Put all living creatures
in the light.

Put all living creatures
in the light.
Expand the Light
to the limits of the Universe
and beyond all space and time.
See all as light.

65. When you see all as One,
you have entered
a state of meditation.
Remove the hardness
that smothers your Light.
"Cast off the works of darkness
and put the armour of Light".

Seeing all as light becomes
your most challenging
and important task.
"God is Light."

How long should I pray each time?

66. Continue your daily prayers
for as long a period
as you enjoy.
Your fifteen minutes sessions
will gradually grow
to one hour or more.
Pray deeply and systematically.
Every minute spent
in prayer
and meditation
brings you closer to God.

Will daily prayer help me
to overcome bad habits?

A time will certainly come
when you no longer relish
dark and evil thoughts,
no longer thirst
for underhanded plans
or ill-gotten gains.
You will lose your taste for
dead or toxic foods and drinks.
Your willingness to be involved
in anything which lowers
the state of man
will vanish.
You will not be concerned with
gossip or injury.

How long will it take
for me to merge with God?

67. Your journey will not
be completed in a few minutes
simply because
you want it so.
Entry into God's Kingdom
is the result of long years
of spiritual practice.

I hate to wait.
Is there not a quick way to God?

68. See God's Hand
in everrything that happens;
then you will not become elated, depressed
or be impatient.
Your life will be
a continuous experience of God.
You will live
in the divine realm with Jesus,
know the peace beyond words
and see all
as God's Everlasting Light.
"God is Light
and in Him
There is no darkness at all".

How may I best serve God
and help mankind?

69. First you must experience God.
For you
nothing is as genuine
as your own experience.
To experience God in your life,
you must see mankind as God.
Take up work
which is dedicated to God
and your fellow man.
Practice, don't preach.
"Do unto others
what you wish them
to do unto you".
Do not do to others
what you do not wish them
to do to you.
Do not have a double standard.
Treat everyone
as your own self.

You must have faith in yourself
in order to have
faith in others.
You must respect
both yourself and others.
Mankind is one community.
Harm yourself
and you weaken all.
Hurt another
and you lose your strength.
The treatment that you
wish others to give you
is the measure
of your duty to them.

Individual fulfillment
comes only
through serving others.

What is the best way to serve
others?

70. First remould your own character.
     Then make your home
     a haven of God's Love.
     Then improve your neighbourhood,
     city, nation
     and the world.
     You have to show by example
     that the path of Jesus
     is the path to perfect joy.
     You have a great responsibility:
     Your courage,
     unselfishness
     and conviction
     under all circumstances
     lets others realise
     that the hours
     that you have spent
     in spiritual practice
     have made you
     a better,
     happier,
     more constructive person.
     Prayer and the spiritual life
     are not things you carry on
     only when you are hidden
     from public view.
     They are
     a twenty-four-hour-a-day
     occupation.

     It is your duty to God
     and your Soul
     to pray, contemplate,
     meditate,
     so as to move closer to Him.

71. The body God gave you
     must be usefully employed
     in order to maintain
     good health,
     so that you may make good use
     of His Gift
     of physical life.
     Do not mock Him
     by becoming lazy
     or wayward.

What are character faults?
How should they be overcome?

72. A character fault
is anything in your nature
which distracts from
or obstructs
the path to God
either for you or
others.
Good character is
a manifestation
of the Soul.

How are character faults created?

73. The mind and senses
get into a mire of desire and frustration.
We see someone
who has a new car.
Suddenly we begin to want
not only his car,
but a car which
our minds tell us
will be better than his.
Does all this bring us closer to God?
According to the Bible,
Jesus 1 told us,
"It is easier for a camel
to pass through
the eye of a needle
than for a rich man
to enter the Kingdom of God" *Mt. 19:24*

Does this mean that
the people of the Earth's
wealthier nations
have no chance for salvation?

Not necessarily,
but it does mean
that to live as Jesus lived,
and as He asks
all of us to live,
we must be very careful
to control
our desires
for things which distract us
from God.

74. Our stature
in God's eyes
depends upon the extent
of our character reform.

The wandering
of our untrained senses
and minds
creates emotional enemies
to our spiritual work.
If we give our hearts
to these weaknesses,
there will be no room
for God.
When we sit quietly
for prayer
where will our attention be?
On distractions
which take us from God:
anger, greed,
lust, envy,
grief, pride,
fear, egoism and hatred.
These names are given
to some of our personal weaknesses.
Which of us is
completely free of them?

Do we have to conquer desire
to be good Christians
and follow Jesus?

75. How can we become
stronger spiritually
while we dissipate the Love
God gives us,
trying to satisfy
the unrest,
anxiety and worry,
created by our
unrestrained sense cravings
and unholy emotions?

76. Can the dove of peace
and the serpent of Satan
live happily in the same person?

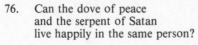

Divine Love,
discipline,
virtue and compassion,
which are the foundations
of good character
cannot develop
until we overcome
the evil tendencies
of the mind.
Jesus 1 had to face
the temptations of the Devil
for forty days
before He began
his teaching mission.
We must follow His example
and conquer the inner devils
before we begin
to give ourselves fully
to the service of others.

Must we cultivate restraint?

77. Many of us today
say and do anything
which comes into our heads.
We have lost contact
with conscience,
morals
and godly conduct.
Wise advice leaves the
fully corrupt
unchanged.
Only when we see
a weakness in our characters
can we take steps to
remove it.

How exactly
do bad emotions arise?

78. Humans are born
with an endowment
of spiritual power
and love.

Children are not given
education in
the proper use of the senses.
The children grow up
with undisciplined habits.
The senses
wander to any attractive,
exciting
or stimulating activity or object.

The mind becomes filled
with random thoughts
about enticing
or upsetting things.
When we look at the world,
our spiritual energies
flow through the thoughts
we have accumulated.
Desires arise.

79. Things are slow to happen.

As we want things quickly,
lust and impatience
grow within us.

Next we become angry.
Anger arises
either
because we have what we wanted
but don't like it,
or because we didn't get
what we wanted.
So we blame someone else
for the situation.

80. If we have what we want,
we become afraid
that we may lose it.
If we don't have it,
we fear
that we may not get it.

As life continues
some desires
are not fulfilled.

We become disappointed
and feel loss and grief.
Later
we see someone else
who has something,
so we feel envy.
Envy leads to greed and hatred.
Our hard emotions
make us grow narrow,
intolerant and prejudiced.
Finally,
if something does come our way,
we feel proud.

How do we prevent
this unhappy chain of events?

81. Control your senses.

How is this control exercised?

Start with you eyes —
your eyesight.
Each time you see
something which stirs your mind,
look at a picture of Jesus 1 instead
or concentrate on what you are doing.
Soon you will begin
to feel at peace.
It may take time, so
just work away at it
little by little.

82. The errors of the tongue
will give you the most trouble.
The tendency toward spreading scandal
and sensual conversation
is strong.
Say very little.
When there is a pressing need
to speak,
speak gently.
Do not shout
or raise your voice
in anger,
or excitement.
Your health
and social relationships
will improve.
You may be laughed at
as a kill-joy,
but the type of joy
you crave
can never die.

Use your tongue
to repeat the Lord's name.
He will help you tame it.

I have a troubled mind.
What can I do about it?

83. Tame your mind
by serving the Lord.
Prayer
and contemplation of Divinity
go a long way
toward creating
peace of mind.

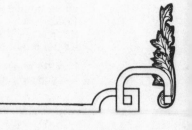

Discipline,
restraint
and good judgement
are the right remedies
for character weaknesses
which mar our daily lives.

Doesn't good discipline
require will-power?

84.	God is Love.
Love is God's power.
Will power
motivated by God's Power
is the active force
available for your uplift.
Let your life
become a manifestation
of Divine Will.
Don't let the mind
lead you along the wrong path.

85.	According to Matthew 26:41
Jesus 1 said,
"Watch and pray
so that you may not
enter into temptation ..."
WATCH:
W-atch your words;
A-watch your actions,
T-watch your thoughts,
C-watch your character;
H-watch your heart.
Today we look to
a different type of watch.
At least let your watch
remind you of these requirements.
Don't watch temptation
— W A T C H.

Sometimes I need help, but
no one is present.

86.	God is never absent.
The simpliest prayer
to remember in times of need
is "Je'su, Je'su, Je'su ..."
After a time
you won't forget it.
Jesus is never absent.
The same Jesus 1
is in all of us.
Look for Him in others.

To hate another
is to hate God
and the Jesus
you love so well.
We are each forms of
God's Love.

How is jealousy overcome?

87.   The one you inflict pain on
with your envy,
is you, yourself,
with another name.
Give up envy.
A contented person is free.

Become aware of
your own present capabilities.
Beyond your limits
you find stress,
upset, over burdening
or even personal degradation.
Do not become jealous of
those who are more gifted.
Hold firmly
to the spiritual procedures
which cause your Soul
to grow stronger
and more useful
to God.

What about nervousness and
impatience with people?

88.   Deliberately breathe slower
and more deeply.
Stay calm.
Repeat the Lord's name
and look for God
in each person
whom you see.

Fear, rivalry,
lust, greed, pride,
egoism and envy
will disappear.
Rejoice
when another person is happy.
Such an attitude pleases
the Lord.
God is the father of all, so
try to be a good brother
or sisiter
to each of His children.

89.   Don't let impatience
or any other emotion
cause you to fall
from the divine level
to the animal level.
Ask yourself
"What would Jesus [1]
do in this situation?"
Extend patience
and understanding.
Look at the "other person".
Try to discover
a point of contact,
not a point of conflict.
Use your knowledge
to make yourself kinder.
Don't worry about failure;
Life will become worth living.

Morality and discipline,
though they may seem
unpleasant at first
lead to a happy life.

What are the best remedies
for anger?

90.   Anger comes from lust.
Not all lust however is sensual:
Any strong unreasoning desire
for something is lust.
Someone may say something
which provokes you.
Do your best
to be calm and sweet.
Say "I'm surprised
that my behaviour
has given you that impression."
Smile.
Do not take it to heart.

Remind yourself
that even Jesus [1]
had to withstand attack.

91.   If you live in
an atmosphere of anger
and still retain your virtue,
you have made a noteworthy achievement.
Your calmness denotes
your spiritual advancement.

Try to suppress
the first traces of anger
that you see in yourself.
Usually anger does not
come upon you without warning:
your body becomes warm,
the lips twitch, and
the eyes redden or tighten.

92. The anger may increase,
but do not act rashly.
Repeat the name of the Lord
until you overcome the anger;
drink a glass of cold water,
sip it slowly;
cool down;
sit alone for a while
in a comfortable position
or lie down in bed
until the upset passes,
and you laugh
at your temporary insanity.

93 In anger you become a drunken brute
and abuse others;
they do the same, and
tempers rise.
The harmful vibrations released
can injure your body permanently.
Can you afford to become
a wild beast?

94. Experiment with
the remedies for anger.
They may seem difficult at first,
but you have to practise.
Years of repenting
may never repair
the damage done
in five minutes of anger.

95. If anger grips you
despite all your efforts,
stay one step ahead of it.

Direct it towards your own
bad habits.
Be angry at your own weaknesses
and bad habits.
Hate them
until you ward off
the evil temper
which stalks you.

This response does not involve
or lead to
self-punishment.
It does involve
self-control,
inner honesty
and a sincere
effort to improve.

What is the answer
to grief?

96. Do not grieve as others do.
Never be depressed
and brood over the past.
When grief overwhelms you,
do not dwell on
similar losses from the past
and add to your sorrow.
Turn your attention to the
times when you were happy.
Concentrate on this activity for a time.
Call on the good Lord
by name
as you relive your past joys.
Be consoled
by the past;
do not be dragged down
into the depths of self-pity
or sadness for your plight.

97. You are treading Jesus ı path.
When your mental
and emotional reactions
have been transformed
into Divine Love,
everything that you are aware of
will take on a divine quality.
You will be shaped in
a mould of Love.
Because your every action
will be divine,
you will be able to
live in the world
and yet be undisturbed by it.

Keep the mind
filled with Love and
all will go well.

What care do we need to give
to the body?

98.   Let the food you eat
be transformed into good deeds,
good thoughts
and kind words.
Act,
but do not cause others pain
or add to their misery.
God's Love creates good health.
Live
so that your every breath
takes you closer to God.
Don't miss meals.
Be regular in your habits.
Those who eat too much
become exhausted.
The weak and undernourished
are unfit to serve mankind.

99.   Preserve your health,
Physical illness
can be a great handicap
to your divine growth.
The body
will refuse to be ignored.
It will distract you
from your spiritual work.
Divine Love prevents all disease.
Use the body,
its strength and capabilities
to serve others
with love and humility,
to sincerely worship the Lord,
to sing His glory,
to visit holy places,
to keep the senses away from
the wrong path
and to tread
the path of God.

100.   Do work
which expands your interests.
Dedicate
both the activity and the results
to God.
Share your joy,
skill and knowledge
with your fellow-man.

Won't these practices require inner discipline?

101.   Discipline
is the first step
on the path to God.
Today many people
who cannot tolerate
even minor difficulties
and inconveniences
crave rapid spiritual advancement
and immediate higher consciousness.

102.   Self-control
allows spiritual power
to increase safely.
Your good character
ensures that power
will be beneficially used.
Your self-discipline
will lead you to happiness.
To concentrate on developing
the discipline you need
is far more important,
than to be concerned with
quick results.

103.   Discipline does not involve
force or needless hardship.
Never try to force your mind.
It will respond easily
to tenderness
and patient training.

104.   Treat your wandering mind
like a small child;
bring up your child
by training it
to become wiser
and wiser;
caress it into good ways.
Don't be hasty.
Slowly and steadily
coax yourself away from
bad company
and join the company
of good people [3]
or sit alone with God!
This action must be taken
to master the mind.

105.   If you constantly feed on
the poison of bad influences,
how can you recover?

What are the stages we progress through
to achieve self-control?

106.   The first step
       is control of the senses.
       Curb the temptation
       to experience degrading things.

107.   The second
       is control of the emotions
       and compelling urges.
       Let them run if they must,
       but don't let them take
       the body with them.
       Don't let low urges motivate
       base actions.

108.   The third step
       involves the development
       of balanced judgement
       and even-mindedness.
       You must learn to be
       unbiased
       and free from prejudice.

109.   Next
       you must learn to regulate
       the vital energies
       of the mind,
       the body and the spirit.
       Jesus 1 demonstrated such control
       when He turned to see
       who had touched
       the hem of His robe.
       You must become just as
       aware as Jesus was of
       the movements of
       the Love God gives you.

110.   The fifth step involves
       the formation of
       a divine buffer
       between you
       and outside influences
       that would distract you
       from God.
       Jesus 1 envelops you
       with His divine protection.
       "You put on the armour of Light."

111.   Next you will develop
       single-mindedness
       or "singleness of heart" —
       Nothing can pull you
       away from God.

112.   In the seventh stage
        meditation on
        "the Unity of God in all existence"
        will intensify
        and lead you
        to awareness of Unity with God. —
        The eighth and final stage
        there,
        you and the Father are One.

113.   Meditation is far above
        sensory organs.
        You will recognize this stage
        when you lose
        all awareness of the meditator,
        the act of meditation
        and the object of meditation.

        You merge into
        an awareness of Unity,
        Love and Light.
        Nothing can be
        as genuine for you
        as your own experience
        which makes all discipline
        worthwhile.
        Early divine experiences
        hint at the unequalled majesty
        of the everlasting
        embrace of God,
        which is your goal.

        How can balanced judgement
        be developed?

114.   Sound judgement
        requires good discipline.
        Meditation alone
        will clarify your vision.
        With good vision
        you will easily see
        which thoughts
        are good ones,
        which words
        are valuable to say
        and which action
        should be carried out.

115.   One
        very bad habit deserves
        your special attention.

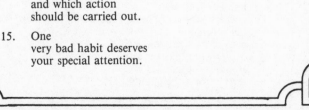

Whenever you
have the opportunity
to carry out some action
which is exciting,
even though you know
that it is not good,
you are very quick
to do it.
Yet whenever
you see the opportunity
to do something
which you know to be good,
you become extremely cautious
and hesitant.
You say, when asked to do something good,
"I don't have time now.
I cannot concentrate."
But you always have time
and energy
for things which you know
are not virtuous.
This habit must be reversed.
Good activities must be encouraged:
bad ones shunned.

116.   It may take years
of patient discipline
and prayer
to correct one wrong action.
Consider the consequences
of your words
and action.
Serve the common good.
Haste makes waste.

Why do I worry so much?

117.   Most daily concerns
which worry us
are passing fancies.
If pursued,
They add nothing
to the spiritual value
of our lives.
So don't be in a hurry.

118.   Immerse yourself
in the vastness of God's Glory.
Let this larger,
more important concern
overpower the lesser attractions.
If you must worry,
worry about the quality

of your devotion
To the Lord.
Consider the strength
of your discipline
in His eyes.
If you must yearn for something,
yearn for the beauty of His smile.

Does talking things over
with people improve judgement?

119. Talk less.
Think more deliberately.
Try to see
what is truly important.
It is your mission
to follow the Lord's ways
with as few deviations
as possible.

120. If you are not sure
of what action you should take,
pray and meditate
for a half-hour or more
until the right path
becomes obvious.
The reason for uncertainty
stems from our concentration
on the most minute bodily
or physical needs
and emotional desires,
with no regard for
the Lord's requirements.
Just as Jesus 1
sacrificed His Body
for the salvation
of mankind,
we must rise above
the tendencies of the flesh
and the desires of the emotions
in order to honour
the God within.

121. Most things
are of no lasting value.
Use your good judgement
to tell the tinsel
from the gold,
the passing from the
permanent,
the gaudy from
the godly,

the momentary
from the everlasting,
the distracting
from the Divine.
Don't be afraid
to stop something
you have started
if you realize
that it is wrong.
Use whatever judgement
you have
to the best of your ability;
so as to gradually
increase the strength
and quality
of your judgement.

Why do I feel
no sense of conscience,
just confusion?

122. Ask yourself
what pleases God
Strive to do your best;
your conscience will awaken
to give you direction.
Take it as a guide;
don't brush it aside
whenever the urge arises
to go the other way.

Why am I so impulsive?

123. If you let your mind
attach itself
to every physically exciting idea,
where will your judgement lie?

Don't be led
into wrong activity;
keep your word;
practice what you preach;
speak from the bottom of your heart;
follow your own conscience,
not unrestrained urges
which are the source of all sin.
Let emotions go.
See with loving eyes
Experience truth;
walk the straight and steady path.
God will be with you
every step of the way.

What particular outlook
on life can help me
to improve my character,
my self-discipline,
my good judgement,
and help me to be happy?

124. Humans often feel
that they are very cultured,
hightly evolved,
and advanced.
If we take the trouble to look,
much can be learned
from the ways of the tiny ants.

What can be learnt from ants?

125. Do not neglect
the gifts you have
You have a human body
with divine capabilities.
When your attention is free,
give it to God.
Repeat Jesus' 1 name.
Never weaken yourself

by thinking of yourself
as hopeless, bad, inferior
or someone who "doesn't count".
No Soul is worthless.

Ants are constantly
absorbing themselves
in useful work
for the good of their group.
Take up
or continue doing
a useful job in your life.
As a true Christian, 1
the spiritual group
that you should identify with
is made up of people who
are ready to make any
sacrifice
to grow nearer to God.
They as Jesus 2 did,
serve only God,
and no lesser interests.
You must serve
this group of people
who are struggling to be good
in a difficult atmosphere.

126. Ants quietly do
      their duty
      and by steady activity
      accomplish much.
      Look at everything
      with penetrating,
      calm judgement.
      You always
      have enough concentration
      to do things which
      distract you from God.
      So now you must
      acquire the habit of
      turning toward God.
      Progress will be
      slow and stead,
      but God-ward direction
      is your aim.

      Why do I suddenly feel strong
      and then later feel weak?

127. Quick bursts of power and lights
      may distract you.
      Even in the best of times
      we must not
      forget our discipline.
      After a strong upsurge in spirit
      you may feel discouraged
      if it does not
      happen again soon.
      Take rising spiritual experiences
      as samples of the
      good to come.
      Do not forget
      or deliberately neglect
      the long hours
      of painstaking prayer
      and discipline
      which gave you
      the gift of God's Grace.

      What else can we learn from ants?

128. Ants never selfishly
      hoard.
      Like ants,
      we should not consider
      that the temporary luxuries
      we have at our disposal
      are ours to hoard
      or misuse.

God is everywhere
and in everything.
To waste anything
is to waste God.
Prosperity is ours to use
for the good of mankind.
"More property"
means God expects us to
do more for mankind.

He didn't
give us a new car
so that we can feel proud
because we could outrun
the local police.
Every act of yours
either takes you
nearer to the Lord,
or away from Him.

129.   Ants do not lose heart
when obstacles arise
or changes occur.
They simply do their best.
God takes care of the rest.
Your actions are responsible for your progress
or your decline.
When you do
an act for Jesus,[1]
let Jesus decide
upon the result.
If you have asked Him for work,
you have to accept
His control of the outcome.
What you receive
and when you receive it
depends upon His Grace.
If the outcome doesn't turn out
to be what you were expecting
but your spirits
remain buoyant,
that is a valuable achievement.
Simply do your best,
God does all the rest.

What other good traits do ants have?

130.   Ants are never
seen excitedly chasing
a fit of passion.
God's wages
are your good qualities.

So if you want cash
instead of virtue
why are you following Jesus?

Why don't I always care to do
what must be done?

131.   If you have to fill a role
which seems distasteful,
do it out of love.
Then you may stop
at the time
which seems right to you.
When your mind seems compelled
to look into certain activities,
do your best
to see God there.
Ask yourself,
"How is Jesus working through me here?
This work is a manifestation
of God:
how can I see God in it?
For what reasons do
I often feel critical?"

132.   Look for the areas
in your conduct
which need improvement.
Don't waste time
trying to highlight others' weaknesses.
Share their joys,
encourage them
and direct them toward God
in their times of trouble,
but let Jesus ₁
take care of them
in His way.
Don't enforce your will
on others
or think that you alone
are responsible
for their welfare.
If you are solely in charge,
what is God's role?

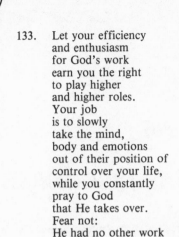

133. Let your efficiency
and enthusiasm
for God's work
earn you the right
to play higher
and higher roles.
Your job
is to slowly
take the mind,
body and emotions
out of their position of
control over your life,
while you constantly
pray to God
that He takes over.
Fear not:
He had no other work
than to lovingly watch over
and nurture His children.

134. May you close the vast gap
between:
what you are capable of doing,
and what you are presently accomplishing.
May you "lead a life
worthy of God,
who calls you
into His own Kingdom
and glory." *1Thess. 2:12*
May your life be well spent.
May you know God's Love.

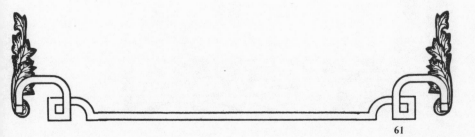

1976

SAI CHRISTMAS DISCOURSE

"The Flowering of Divinity"

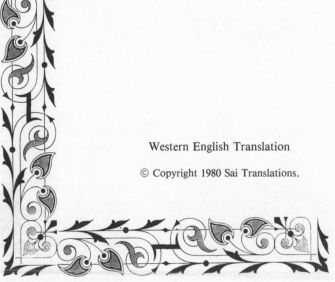

Western English Translation

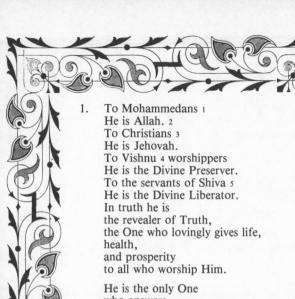

1. To Mohammedans 1
    He is Allah. 2
    To Christians 3
    He is Jehovah.
    To Vishnu 4 worshippers
    He is the Divine Preserver.
    To the servants of Shiva 5
    He is the Divine Liberator.
    In truth he is
    the revealer of Truth,
    the One who lovingly gives life,
    health,
    and prosperity
    to all who worship Him.

    He is the only One
    who answers
    when we call God's name.
    He exists
    before the beginning of creation.
    He is the sustainer
    of all existence.
    He continues
    when all things cease to be.
    In Sanskrit
    His name is Bhagavan.

2. Embodiments of living God,
    Each human is the seed of Divinity.

    A tiny seed
    is planted in the earth.
    It gradually grows
    from a tender sprout
    into a delicate leafy plant.
    Finally it becomes
    a tremendous tree.
    Every Soul
    who is given a human body
    has the opportunity to grow,
    stage by stage,

    into fully evolved
    Divinity.

3. Two wheels
   make a platform
   into a cart
   which may travel far.

   Two strong wings
   allow a fledgling bird
   to soar
   into the heavens.

4. Without two wheels
   will a wooden platform
   move at all?
   Can it be called a cart?

   Without two wings
   will a feathered body
   fly into the heavens
   and glorify the world
   with its song?
   Can it be called a nightingale?

5. Our human bodies
   will transform into living channels
   for Divinity
   to pour through
   if we have two
   kinds of knowledge.

6. We need worldly knowledge
   and Higher Knowledge.

7. Worldly knowledge
   allows us to maintain
   our physical bodies.

8. To open
   the doorway to God,
   we need knowledge of
   the Higher
   aspects of Life.

9. Knowledge of the physical world
   gives us the means
   to earn a living.

   Knowledge of God
   clearly lights the way
   to the goal of living.

10. Worldly knowledge relates to
    sustaining a physical body
    long enough
    and well enough for us
    to perceive and reach
    the goal of life.

11.   Food gathering
and continuously accumulating
more and more
material items
is not the goal of life.

Human beings
do not come to Earth
merely to gather
the physical necessities
for bodily life.

12.   Why have we all come
into this world?
What is the world?
Who created it?
What is the goal
of our lives?

This world was created by God
from His essence
so that we can accomplish
the goal of life:
to search for
and achieve
Divinity.

13.   The purpose of every religion
is to reveal
the true goal of life.

No religion is merely
a list of techniques
for earning a living.

14.   Every person
has the basic need
to go through the struggle
necessary
to grasp Divinity.
After many trials
we must learn
to look to Divinity
for our every need.
We must bring
the essence of God
into man.
That is the true
goal of life.

15.   To please God
we have to become living examples
of Divine principles.

16. The gradual training
God gives us
in these principles
requires discipline
we call it
spiritual discipline.

17. If you move against
Divine Law,
you are moving against God
and you are bound to fail.

You are moving against
life's basic nature,
your life becomes
living death,
and at some point
this wrong action
will have to stop.
Mankind as a whole,
and indeed
all living things,
will perish
if the Divine Natural Laws
for sustaining life
are too greatly violated.
Many primitive animals
and human forms
no longer exist
on earth today
for this reason.

18. Living conditions on Earth
are constantly changing.
The essentials
to maintain life
change.
To meet the needs
of different ages,
God sends sages
and Divine Incarnations 1
to sustain
human life on Earth.
These living examples
of Divine Law
lead ideal lives
and guide humanity
in the disciplines needed
to live according to
the Divine Plan
for each Age.

19. What is needed today
is not a new society,
not a new form of education,
not a new religion.
Today
humanity must move to
a much higher level of
inner mental purity.
Purity of consciousness
must be achieved
if man is to survive.

20. Humanity is trapped
under a huge stone —
the unholy burden
of ego.
Envy, hatred and selfishness
dominate the life styles
of most humans today.
Evil
will not prevail!
Love
must shine forth!
Each individual
must free himself
of the burden of
selfish interest.
Then at last
human society
will rise to its own
natural level —
the Divine level

21. To become truly human
you must recognize
and understand
the true nature of
the relationships
between individuals.
You must experience
the natural Divinity
that exists
between all people.
You must take
a broader view.
You must cultivate
divine relationships
between father and son,
mother and daughter,
brother and brother,
sister and sister
social group,

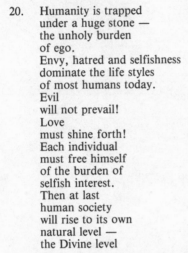

rich
and poor,
the educated
and the illiterate,
between country
and country.
Love must not be abandoned.
You must find Love.

22. To reach the divine shores,
people of today's world
must travel beyond
the illusory differences
which separate them.
We have become
individuals
weakly defending
defined personal domains
much as animals do.
We each must rise
above the narrow limits
of self-interest.
We must become Love,
and expand as Love
to completely fill
all the limits of Life.
Grasp
the scope of God's Love.
Be transformed
into the godly world
of infinite
Divine Consciousness.

23. Outgrow the boundaries
of the individual.
Become the full nature of
your True Self.
Your relationship
with the wide
external world
will become obvious.
You will forget
narrow self-interest
and know the unending joy
of living and breathing in
the fullness
of God's creation.

24. There is no way
for humans to exist
without the life support
this wide spacious world
gives us.

25. A minute droplet
    of salt water
    will soon dry up
    and disappear
    when it is removed from
    the vast ocean.

26. That same water droplet
    is referred to
    as the Pacific Ocean
    when it coexists
    as part of the vast
    Pacific Ocean.

27. Who would
    call the tiny droplet of water
    the Pacific Ocean
    when it separates from the ocean,
    and attempts short-lived,
    independent existence?
    The potential fullness of its identity
    is lost.

28. We each have value
    when we are fully functioning parts
    of our vast ocean,
    the external world we live in.

29. All people,
    to be truly human,
    should see themselves as
    the living Truth
    which pervades the entire world
    we call external.

30. It is never a person's duty
    to cultivate competitive self-interest,
    prejudice and hatred,
    in himself or others.

31. When minute droplets
    are released into a mighty ocean,
    their substance gradually expands
    and can never be removed
    from the ocean again.
    When the very basis of
    that which makes us feel
    separate from others
    is dissolved,
    and merges with universal Divinity,
    we become God-minded
    and know infinite,
    eternal life.

32. Each one of us
     must develop a broad heart,
     a godly outlook
     and purity of thought.

33. When we each have
     broadened and purified our
     strength of character and consciousness,
     each country of the world
     and the entire globe
     will know Divine Peace
     and Infinite Joy.

34. Today
     is a very sacred day.
     Today
     is the Birthday
     of Jesus Christ. 1

35. When Jesus existed
     in human form
     His first announcement was,
     "I am God's Messenger".2

36. Jesus was not the only Messanger
     sent by God.
     We each come into
     this world
     as a Messenger
     sent by God. 1

37. Each and every human being
     born on Earth
     comes into this world
     with the same mission.
     Your purpose
     is to reveal
     the great secret of life.
     You must uncover the sacredness
     which is the true nature of life
     and share infinite beauty
     with humanity.

38. You did not become a member
     of the human race
     to spend all your waking hours
     running
     from one selfish craving to another.
     You were not
     put here to use
     all your precious time
     earning a living.

39. To accomplish your life's mission
you must first know
why you have become human.
Your highly evolved human body
is a tool with which you
may view the Infinite
and proclaim God's true power
and divine capabilities
to the world.
With your living example,
the mysteries of God
will become more evident
to all humanity.

40. The true nature
of every person
is a dazzling light
of Divinity.
You should radiate
God's sacred nature
every second of the day.

41. Where is God?
God is not restricted.
He is not
available only in caves
or on high mountain tops.
He is not
hiding in the East or
in brightly lit Western cities.
He did not die
thousands of years ago.
You need not wait
thousands of years
for Him to come.

42. He is ever present
in every human heart.

43. If you crave to see God,
if you truly yearn
for a vision
of the ultimate Divinity,
you need not have been born
in another time.
There is no need
to leave your home
and travel to some far-away place.

44. Without question you will see God.
You need only begin to
withdraw your attention from
the excitement of the physical world.

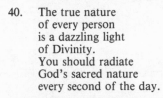

Focus ever more fully
within your being.
When you have done this
you will know Divinity.
You will experience
God's overwhelming Love.
You need never doubt this.

45.   In the "The Song of God",
the Bhagavad Geeta, 1
written in the Indian religious language,
Sanskrit, 2
it is clearly stated:
"God, who shines brighter than
one hundred thousand suns,
shines
in your heart."
Yet you
forget God
and spend all your time
submerged in the ignorance
of the external world.

46.   The most ancient poetry
availabloe on Earth today
is found in the Vedas 1 of India.
These chanted verses
of timeless wisdom
say,
"Know you are
the child of immortality."

47.   Humans
neglect this wisdom
and assume that
they are only bodies.
Convinced of this illusion,
you suffer and weaken
under the burden of
countless worries about physical concerns.

48.   The oldest written Scriptures
still in existence,
the Indian books of Truth —
the Vedas, 1
describe you as
"the embodiment of immortal Truth,
infinite Divine Consciousness
and unending Bliss".
Do you
try to discover Truth
and Bliss
in yourself?

Or do you instead
constantly whimper along,
feeling dejected and sorry
about your imaginary weakness?

49. All the problems
that you have today
stem from three basic sources.
You have forgotten God,
shining bright than one thousand suns,
within you.
You have forgotten
that you
are the child of immortality.
You have forgotten
that you
are the living embodiment of Bliss.
You suffer
all the worries
of the physical world
because of your ignorance
about your Divinity.
You ignore
your true nature.

50. You become human
to shine with God's briliance
in the world.
You wear
a body
which will one day die.
To show all
that you never die,
your body walks
in the troubled world
to give forth the message
that you are infinite Bliss.
These are the messages
God sent you to deliver.

51. To say,
"I am a bread winner,
I live to eat and sleep"
is the height of ignorance.

Your mission is
to drive out ignorance
and keep it far away.
You live in this world
to prove the true nature
of the God within you
by your ideal conduct
in every situation.

From your behaviour
others will recognize
the true nature of life
and set out to achieve
life's true purpose.

52. You are embodiments of Divine Spirit.
All birds
eat,
sleep,
mate,
multiply
and react to fear.
Is that why
you are here?

53. Among all types of living bodies,
only a human body
allows a being access to
the three types of wisdom.
While you
have a human body
you can master the physical sciences.
You can expand your scope
to the science of spiritual betterment.
You can work consistently
until you experience God,
and become
the fountain of infinite knowledge
that He is.
In spite of this divine opportunity,
people spend their days
desiring sleep
or idleness.
Or they dissipate their resources
pursuing sense cravings
by over-eating
and unrestrained sensual behaviour.
They lose their emotional balance
due to unreasoning fear.
Any animal
can live like this.
Do you
live like a human?

54. Do you truly need to study long hours
to obtain technical knowledge?
Is it necessary
to spend many years
at college
and receive university degrees
to adopt
the life-style
of illiterate animals?

55. If you live
     like an animal,
     why have a human body?
     What good is a human body?
     Are you the same as an animal?

56. No! No!
     You are not the same as
     an animal.
     Divine Truth
     and Love
     are the basic nature of
     each human.
     You are capable of
     the highest sacred conduct
     in accordance with Divine Law.
     Your role in life
     is far beyond
     animal capabilities.
     To be granted human birth
     is much more difficult
     than being born as
     an animal.

57. Because Jesus 1 knew
     the value of being human,
     He lived His life
     as God's Messenger. 2
     Seeing His won Divinity,
     He also saw the Divinity
     in every other person.
     Jesus 1 knew
     that to serve God
     in each individual
     is to serve society.
     To serve society
     is to serve God directly.
     After selflessly serving humanity
     for some years,
     He realized
     that He was
     something far beyond
     His body —
     far beyond physical life or death.
     He realized Himself
     to be the child of immortality —
     the Son of God. 2

58. Since He identified Himself
     fully with God,
     the divine qualities of God
     manifested through Him
     for the benefit of all humanity.

59. If you
wish to blossom forth
as your true Self,
your Higher Divine Nature,
you must spend
the life given you
serving humanity
with great humility
and no concern
for selfish gain.

60. Once Jesus
gave Himself fully
to the sacred service
of all mankind,
He realized
that He was
serving the world.
in human form,
as God
serves the world
When speaking to others,
He described His state saying,
"I
and My Father
are One." [1]

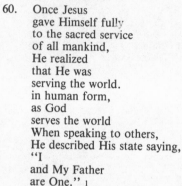

61. When we call ourselves
"Children of God",
it is a poor joke.
We carefully avoid
godly behaviour.
We destroy
any hope of Him being known
for our good character.
Instead
we work diligently
to perfect our bad qualities
and frequently delight in
exaggerated stories
of our misdeeds.

62. If you
wish to be worthy of
the name
"Child of God",
you must at least
make the attempt
to take on God's nature
and grow closer
to God.

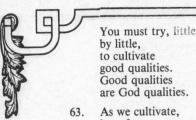

You must try, little
by little,
to cultivate
good qualities.
Good qualities
are God qualities.

63. As we cultivate,
long for,
and nurture
godly qualities,
one by one,
we gradually
come to know more fully
God's true nature.
When we know
God's divine nature completely,
we are One with God.
There is no difference
between ourselves
and God.

64. In India
the divine nature of life
has been described
by three different
spiritual philosophies.
One relates to striving
to be a worthy servant
of God.
A follower of this philosophy
feels that God
is watching his every action.
He knows
how very important it is
to learn how to please God.
This philosophy
is known as
the state
where two exist —
the servant
and God.
A person's world
has two things in it —
oneslef
and God.
One's world is dual.
This spiritual philosophy
is called Dualism. 2

As a person serves God
and mankind,
he develops
a much greater understanding
of God's Love,
warmth
and protection.
He eventually realizes
that God
is watching over him
as a loving Father.
He no longer feels separate.
He feels that he
and God
are one family.
He sees all beings
as God's favoured children.
All are members
of one holy family.
This spiritual philosophy
is no longer Dualism.
Where there was separation,
unity now exists.
It is a type of Non-Dualism
called Special Non-Dualism. 2

Later in one's spiritual progress
all imperfect and inferior qualities
vanish.
Only good,
godly qualities
remain.
A person in this state
cannot see where
his personal qualities end
and where
God's qualities begin.
He cannot distinguish between
himself
and God.
He lovingly goes
through the actions of
serving God
in all humanity.
Because he no longer
sees two separate things,
this third philosophy is called
full Non-Dualism. 1
It describes perfect Unity
and Onesness
with God.

66. As a special
personal relationship with God
arises,
the philosophy
of Special Non-Duality 1
comes into being.
Western spiritual philosophy
very clearly describes this state
with the words,
"I am the Son of God". 2

65. The Biblical statement
"I am the Messenger of God" 2
corresponds to
the Indian philosophy
of Dualism. 3
God
and His Messenger
are two separate entities.
Life is a play
with two principal characters —
God
and His Messenger.
The word "dualism"
is very fitting.

67. In these two philosophies
there is a great difference between
the Messenger of God 3
and the Son of God.

68. The Messenger of God 1
is the servant of God.

69. The Son of God 2
has the authority of God.

70. As the Son of God
gradually cultivates,
ever more constantly,
the sacred qualities
of God,
He becomes fully divine.
This state of ultimate Divinity
is described by the sentence
"I and My Father are One". 3
In Eastern spiritual philosophy
this state of Oneness
is called Non-Duality. 3

71.   Every person
      has to progress in life
      from the state of Dualism,
      feeling separate from God,
      to the state of Special Non-Dualism
      as God's trusted child.
      After this the state of Unity
      with the heavenly Father
      must be achieved —
      full Non-Dualism.
      Whoever you may be,
      you must try to grow
      through these stages
      one by one.

72.   I want
      each and every one of you
      to reach the highest
      spiritual state.
      I wish each of you to know
      the joy
      of full Unity with God.

73.   Even the dullest student
      is not willing to spend
      his entire school career
      sitting in the same classroom,
      endlessly repeating
      the first year's work.

74.   Each human
      is born with
      the innate ability to master
      worldly knowledge,
      the knowledge of
      spiritual improvement
      and the knowledge
      realized
      by direct experience of God.

      Even an ignorant
      or backward child
      struggles to move ahead
      into a new class
      each year.
      Yet adult humans
      who have the ability
      to possess infinite knowledge
      attempt
      to stay in the same class
      for an entire lifetime.

What great ignorance
it is to spend an entire lifetime
repeating
various studies of the physical world
and never graduate
to the spiritual
or godly level.

75. As living embodiments
of infinite spirit,
you must attempt
to realize
your full potential.
You must move up
from the narrow-minded idea
that you
are separate from God.
Become
His knowing servant.
Earn the right to be called
the loving Child of God.
Expand
to your fullest capability.
In Eastern philosophical terms,
you must progress
from Dualistic separatism
as God's obedient messenger,
through Special Non-Dualism

as God's Child,
to the Non-Dualistic
state of merger
with God.
You must enjoy
the eternal
Divine Bliss
of knowing Unity
with God.

76. The state of merging with God
in Eastern philosophical terms
is Non-Dualism.
In Christianity 1
God's
acceptance of a person,
and the act of unifying with him
is described by
the Biblical statement,
"He was filled
with the Holy Ghost."

77. So the first step
is to become God's servant, 2
and serve humanity.

The second step occurs
when you become completely absorbed
in divine service.
When you reach the third stage
no barriers remain
between you,
God
and humanity.
All is Love.
All is One.
Your divine hand
is God's Divine Hand.

78. Great emperors
and kings
were proud to rule
vast empires.
Where are the kings
and queens
of the past?
Do they
even in memory,
still exist?

79. Throughout
Earth's long history,
countless Souls
have come into the world
to restore justice
and encourage the prosperity
of humanity.
Does the memory of these people
live in the hearts of all people?

80. The people
who are remembered most
give up all selfish interests,
and take on fully
the divine
selfless service of God
and all humanity.
They lead exemplary lives
and speak the Word of God
to all.
Others follow their example
of self-sacrifice.
The unselfish Love
released by the sacrifice
of selfish interests
is the very nature of God.
We celebrate the Birthdays
of these immortal,
unselfish
Saviours of mankind.

81   The highest
godly quality of the Soul
is present
in all living beings.
It is the highest Truth.
It is our
true nature.
It alone
is always unified
with God.
It is the God
within each of us.

82.   Once you realize that
God is within you,
you naturally
desire to know Him fully.
You crave rest
in the infinite Ocean of Bliss
which is God's Form.
Between you
and infinite Divine Bliss
there are two obstacles.
Two doors must be opened.

83.   These double doors
open and close together.
They block your pathway
to God.
Each door
represents a bad habit.
One door
is the habit
of constantly praising
your own action.
The other door
is blaming others.
These two doors
are bolted together
with the crossbar
of your jealousy.

84.   To reach
infinite Divine Joy,
you must stop
blaming others.
You must stop
inflating yourself
with praise
of your own conduct.
These bad habits
make you feel separate.

They are the doors which block
your path to Divinity.
They must be opened.

85.　Most of us
are moving in the wrong direction.
We constantly blame others
and consistently praise ourselves;
we keep the crossbar
of jealousy
firmly in place
with a huge lock —
our inflated egos.

86.　We must use the divine key
to open the lock
of inflated ego.
The key is Divine Love.

87.　The hands of infinite,
divine peace of mind
must, with the great steadiness of
good character,
gently remove
the crossbar of jealousy.
Then with the key of
Divine Love,
in the gentle hands of
Sacred Peace,
the doors must be
flung wide open.
With the doors of
ego-inflating
self-praise
and the door,
made by blaming others,
pushed out of the way,
you may enter
the infinite Home
of Divine Bliss.

88.　As infinite God
in human form,
consider this:
people today work
very long hours
and make great personal sacrifices
to become known as
educated people,
or to become experts
in various studies.

You may spend
ten years
to master the use
and repair machinery.
You may study for
twelve or fifteen years
to become a government employee.
You may spend
twenty years
trying to get a Ph.D.
If you
wish to please God,
fulfill His purpose
for putting you on Earth.
Live in harmony
with the Divine Law
of the universe.
You must pursue
spiritual education.
It is the only education
of lasting importance.

89. All non-spiritual studies
     are small, twisting streams
     winding their ways
     to the infinite Ocean of
     Perfect Spiritual Knowledge.

90. The final outcome
     of each of these shallow streams
     of worldly education
     is to move you
     a little closer to
     merger with
     the Ocean of Infinite Bliss.

91. A South Indian poet,
     called the "Master of spiritual
     surrender to God's Will", 1
     once wrote:
     "You need not spend your life
     running from river to river,
     trying to cleanse yourself
     with all the waters of the world.
     You need only
     find the spot where
     all rivers meet the sea.
     There you will find
     the small joys
     of all the separate streams combined
     in the unending
     Ocean of Divine Bliss."

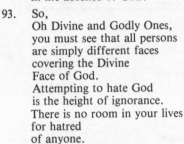

92. Spend your days
     mastering spiritual knowledge.
     All other studies
     are offshoots
     of the one basic Divine Truth
     that you will find
     in the pursuit of spirituality.
     Can anything exist
     in the absence of God?

93. So,
     Oh Divine and Godly Ones,
     you must see that all persons
     are simply different faces
     covering the Divine
     Face of God.
     Attempting to hate God
     is the height of ignorance.
     There is no room in your lives
     for hatred
     of anyone.

94. In the East it is said,
     "All is filled with God."
     This commandment of God's
     was given to Jesus as,
     "All Life is One,
     My Dear Son.
     Be alike to everyone." 1

95. To be truly alive
     you must fill your hearts
     with Divine Love
     and look at all your fellow beings
     with the eyes of Love.
     You must use your love
     to see the same God
     shining through all your fellow beings.

96. There are not countless religions.
     There is only one religion —
     the religion of Divine Love.
     There is only one race —
     the race of mankind.
     There is only one language —
     the language of
     Divine Love in your heart.
     There is only one God.
     He is present everywhere.
     Words alone
     are of no value.
     You must try to
     understand these Truths.

You must gradually
put your Divne Understanding
into practice
in your daily life.
Words without practice
are lies.

97. To see all things as One
you must expand your outlook.
You must
develop a broad Loving Heart.
Selfishness must disappear.
You must
find the greater meaning
of life —
Godliness.
Every spiritual
and religious practice
is a form of striving
to achieve Godliness.
Striving
to lead godly lives
is the only
truly sacred behaviour.

98. Jesus lived
for the Divine Glory of
this sacred planet.
His very action
was for those around Him.
Nothing was too precious
for Him to give up
for His people.
He sacrificed
His body's own blood
for the good of humanity.
Today
is the Birthday
of this Divine Person.
Today
is the anniversary
of the day
when Jesus came to Earth.
Of what meaning is it
to spend such a divine day
feasting?
Is it divine
to spend the entire Birthday of
Jesus,
the master of sense control,
by over-indulging
our own senses?

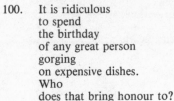

99   Make this day meaningful
and beneficial
for yourself and mankind.
Practice at least a few of the ideals
that Jesus preached
and gave His life for.

100.   It is ridiculous
to spend
the birthday
of any great person
gorging
on expensive dishes.
Who
does that bring honour to?

101.   Celebrate
a true day of rebirth
in your life.
Practice
any ideal
set forth by a great person.
Your divine actions
honour God
who manifested
as the ideal human
you are guided by.

102.   You are embodiments
of living Divine Love.
In memory of Jesus' Birthday,
you must begin to change
your way of living.
You must honor
the living memory of Jesus
by beginning to act
as He acted.
I
wish you
to do this.
From this day onward
do your best
to stop blaming others.
Blame
feeds the fires
of jealousy
and hatred.
From this day forward
stop compulsively praising yourself.
Self-praise
inflates the ego

and moves you
far away from God.
Spend your time
living in the Light
of God's Love.
Employ God's Love
to do God's work.
Shower Love
on all you meet.
Serve the society
you are part of.
Carry on the humanitarian project
that Jesus began.

103.   Today
you invest your God-given energies
in countless diversions.
To explain your actions
you give countless reasons,
some false
and some sincere.
The true motives
for your sick hurry
to do so many things
are often
unknown to you.
All your misdirected busy-ness
cannot help your country.
Selfish interests
do not serve society
or even your own Higher Nature.
You must expand
your view of life.
You must develop
a broader outlook.
Your loving actions
must transform your
ways of thinking.
You must purify
your minds
with Divine Love.
You must become filled with
Selfless Love.
Then will all see
each passing day
as a good day
for every country on Earth.

104.   Some people
put all their efforts
into narrow, self-serving activities,
often at the expense of others.

This not only destroys
the good character of the individual,
it brings shame
on all humanity.
Is this disgraceful behaviour
a worthy product
of your life on Earth?

105. God gave you
an earthly body.
The body He gave you often feels hunger.
The same God
who gave you a hungry body
must provide food
to satisfy your hunger.
God
was fully aware of
your future needs
when he presented you with the body.
He will personally fulfill
the needs of the gift
He gave you
if you trust Him
and allow Him
to care for you.

106. Food
helps keep the physical body alive.
You were not
given your life on Earth
so that you could fill your days
with the struggle
of searching for food.
Earning money for food,
buying food,
cooking food,
eating food,
and thinking about your next meal,
is not your life's work.

107. Try to use your life
to become an ideal
of divine conduct.

108. There is no need
to memorize one hundred thousand divine words
and spout them at all occasions.
You will be better off
if you practice one
of the words you preach.
Your good actions
bring you closer to the ideal
God created you
to establish.

109. The one word
you should live by
is "Love" —
pure,
unselfish
Divine Love.

110. When there is Love
in your heart,
there is God
in your heart.

111. The heart
filled with compassion
is the temple of God.

112. Ancient wisdom holds
that the body
is God's temple.
Your true Divine Nature
is God
living in that temple.

113. You must not use your divine body
to develop bad character.
You must not
set a bad example
for others.
You must make the temple,
your body,
a true place of worship.
Use the body
to serve God.

114. You must experience
Divine Love.
Embrace
the life philosophy
of Divine Love.
I bless you
to go forth
in the service of humanity
and become living examples
of the Love
Jesus showered on humanity.
To celebrate His Birthday,
begin your life's
mission of Love.
Do your best . . . . .

1977

CHRISTMAS DISCOURSE

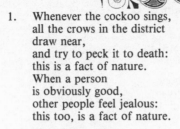

1. Whenever the cockoo sings,
   all the crows in the district
   draw near,
   and try to peck it to death:
   this is a fact of nature.
   When a person
   is obviously good,
   other people feel jealous:
   this too, is a fact of nature.

2. O shining spirits
   of the Divine in human form,
   God has put
   many types of power
   within your reach.

3. The power of your body's muscles,
   the power of skilled hands,
   the power of intelligence,
   the power of influential position,
   the power of scientific knowledge,
   the power to command any situation,
   and the power which God gives you
   when you merge with Him.

4. Each person tries to
   perfect and increase
   his natural powers
   so that, in his own way,
   he may command
   more and more power.

5. Everything comes from God,
   everything is God.
   God created the human race
   as one vast living entity:
   all people are one people;
   all life is One.

6. When people are classified
   according to their actions,
   two categories become obvious:

8. Good people
   always try to do good actions,
   develop only good habits,
   and join only good company.
   They do their good actions
   for the sake of the world.

They knowingly,
or unknowingly,
live in harmony with
Divine Law.
Their lives
are happily dedicated to
the service of others.

9. They try to encourage
anything that will truly
help others.
Good people
feel great joy
when they see others
grow stronger,
physically and spiritually.

10. Bad people find
bad habits,
bad events,
and bad stories
deliciously exciting.
Bad company
is their only pleasure.
They seek out
other bad people,
anywhere
and everywhere they can.
Their evil deeds
are the pride of their lives.

11. They feel irritated by
people who do good for others.
Bad people
become very jealous of
people who work to serve others.
They try to make others
hate good people.

12. Between the good
and the bad,
there is a third group of people —
the middle group.
In India,
and other countries
throughout the world,
Divine Saviours
are sent to Earth by God
to rescue
the middle group of people.

13. Life is like
a vast ocean.

Tides of sorrow
and happiness
constantly rise
and fall.
Many different wave types form,
as the tides of sorrow
and happiness interact.

14. Caught
in the restless seas of life,
man becomes a slave
to constant cravings,
limitless ambitions,
and meaningless emotions.
Lost in these dark
and unnatural waters,
humanity strives ceaselessly
in a hopeless attempt
to acquire things
it is not destined
to have.
From the time he
comes into the world
until he moves into
the next world,
man never knows,
the peace of
his natural state.

15. For humans
who are submerged in
the darkness of unrest,
God sends Divine Torch-bearers
whose Spiritual Light
reveals the proper path
to Divine Destiny.

16. Today we must examine
and attempt to understand
the divine ideals of conduct
which were the signs of
Jesus Christ's 1 Divinity.

17. Jesus' life
was filled with
both extreme virtues
and extreme troubles.
To live
in accordance with
God's natural laws,
Great Souls
must undergo
great hardship

when they come to Earth
to radiate God's Light
and set divine standards
for others to follow.

18. For ordinary human beings also,
every pleasure begins
when some type of **displeasure**
or sorrow ends.
A period of pleasure stops
when **displeasure**
or pain returns.
We may try to ignore
or avoid pain,
or we may try
to fix our attention on
something other than
misery and displeasure,
but we should realize
that by its very nature,
pleasure
is the interval
between two pains;
and similarly
pain
is the interval between
two periods
of pleasure.
Pleasure and ease
can exist
only between two periods
of difficulty or unrest.
We should know that,
if we seek to
enjoy pleasure,
its attractive glow
and captivating appeal
can appear only between
two bad periods
of pain and displeasure.
This is natural law.

19. We are attracted by
the happy periods
in Christ's life
when He was
surrounded by good people.
We grieve over
the times when Jesus
had to suffer pain
and humiliation
at the hands of bad people.

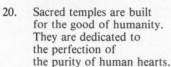

Yet to be very good
one must confront
and deal with
the very bad.
Good cannot exist
without bad.

20. Sacred temples are built
for the good of humanity.
They are dedicated to
the perfection of
the purity of human hearts.

21. To fulfill its sacred mission,
a temple must provide
an atmosphere
which radiates divine harmony.
It must be a place
where good actions,
good practices,
and the good behaviour
of people
are bound together in harmony.
It must demonstrate
that all life
is one sacred harmony.

22. Temples have
a pure, sacred purpose.
Despite this fact,
unholy activities
periodically spring up
within their walls.
This unholiness robs men of
their peace of mind
and distracts them
from God
whom they seek to honour.

23. Money-lending business
were commonplace
in the Temple
in Jerusalem.
Innocent
birds and animals
were sold to be used
as blood sacrifices.
The useless throwing away
of precious lives
mocked God,
their giver of life.

God sent Jesus [1]
to protest against
these evil ways,
and indicate the true path
to Divinity.

24. At that time in Jerusalem,
Jewish [2] religious custom
routinely involved
blood sacrifices
of goats
or other living animals.

25. If a poor Jewish [2] man
could not afford a goat
but wanted to worship,
he hoped
to please God
with a pigeon's death.

26. Jesus Christ [1] saw pigeons
and other animals
being sold
inside the temple.
Money-lenders
shared their profits
with the priests.
Every worshipper
was forced to bring
or buy animals
and join in the slaughter.
No one was spared.
Jesus announced
that bloodshed,
money-lending
and corruption
have no place
in a temple
built in God's name.
He set upon the businessmen
and drove them out of the Temple.
Now that money
was not a part of worship,
He brought the poor,
the troubled,
the orphaned,
and those in need
into the Temple.
He taught them
the pure way to pray
to God
and get relief
from the miseries of life.

27. Certain scholars and priests
felt threatened by Jesus ١.
They envied
His appeal to
common people.
They barred the poor from
the temple
as soon as Jesus
was out of sight.

28. The next day,
when Jesus ١ returned,
a great multitude
of sincere seekers of God
followed Him into the temple.
Jesus received the large gathering
and began to spread God's Word
and show them
the true way
to please God.
The Lord
does not want
innocent birds and animals
killed under terrifying conditions
in a House of God.
How can God,
who is the Ocean
of Infinite Mercy
and Divine Compassion,
be pleased by
needless slaughter
and evil actions?
God is Love.
— Living Love.
He wants
each human
to tread the steady path
of pure,
unblemished,
unselfish Love.
Jesus ١ spoke
very simply and clearly
to the people gathered there.
They realized that
the corrupt priests and scholars
were spreading evil teachings.
They felt
the goodness of God.

29.   The people rejoiced,
      when they heard Him say,
      that our true nature
      is Divine Love
      and Compassion,
      and that each person should
      shower God's Compassion and Love
      on all he sees.
      Jesus 1 told them,
      "All life is One,
      be alike to everyone."
      Extend Love to everyone
      and everything you see.

30.   The priests and scholars
      felt their command of the people
      slipping.
      They knew
      the day would come
      when their wealth,
      possessions,
      and powerful positions
      would all disappear.
      They decided to
      do away with Jesus 1
      before His teachings
      spread further.
      The priests began plotting
      and scheming.
      They made evil plans
      and became possessed
      by evil ideas.

31.   They developed
      the tremendously egoistic **feeling**
      that they would defy God.
      Above all else
      they valued their pride
      and self-importance.
      Hardened by
      their ceremonial butchery,
      the priests thought,
      "We can murder
      and escape suffering for it".
      Such defiance
      is the heights of ego.

Defiance of
the Divine Law of
Universal Justice,
will always cause
a burden of some type
to fall heavily upon us
at some future point.
God cannot be cheated.

32. Whenever pride,
     arrogance,
     selfishness,
     and inflated ego
     enters a person,
     no matter who he may be,
     the Spirit of Love
     in his heart dies,
     and he sinks
     to the lowest level.
     That is the invariable effect
     of self
     inflating ego.
     Whoever it touches
     falls far
     from God's favor.
     To what extent
     do selfish pride
     and ego rule over man today?

33. A particular way
     of looking at things
     may give us the answer.
     Your human bodies
     are very small things
     in a vast universe.

34. If
     out of the entire universe,
     we choose to focus
     our attention on
     this small planet,
     a world map will reveal
     that the country
     we live in, is
     a very small place.

35. Within our country
     the state or province
     in which we live
     appears even smaller.

36. Inside our state,
    our town, city or village
    is much smaller.

37. Our neighbourhood
    is even smaller.

38. Our home
    is far smaller.
    In your home
    how large is your body?

39. Imagine such a
    minute creature
    — a human being,
    prancing about
    blown up with pride,
    almost invisible
    in this vast universe.
    Can it have any validity?

40. A life spent with
    an inflated ego
    is simply a wasted life.
    When we follow ego,
    we waste our lives.
    Waste is the nature of ego.

41. When we knowingly
    or unknowingly,
    allow ourselves
    to become jealous,
    we feel separate from others
    and ego rises within us.
    Feeling separate
    and alone
    is the nature of ego.
    It is the breeding ground of
    all our bad qualitites.

42. You may have
    a very powerful body.
    You may have
    the power of intelligence,
    you may have
    the power of
    advanced education,
    you may have
    the power of
    a high position,
    you may have
    the power of wealth;

many powerful
and influential men
may be willing
to obey you.
All these powers may
make you feel very strong.
But if you do not have
the power of God's Love
moving within you,
each new type of power
you command
will expose new character faults.
You will grow weaker and weaker,
as your grasping for power
reaches out farther and farther.
Power itself is a disease
when it does not
go hand in hand with God.

43. O embodiments of Divine Spirit,
listen well!
All worldly strengths pass away
like clouds blowing in the wind.
They do not last.
The power of God's Love
never fades.

44. There is one sky
above our heads.

45. There is one Earth
beneath our feet.

46. There is only one atmosphere
for us to breath in.

47. There is only one God,
who is the life force
within each of us.

48. How can we call ourselves different?
Where are these differences?
Why do we point out
and pursue differences?

49. Seeing all things
as separate and different
is the basic nature of ignorance.
The more clearly we see all as One,
all as God's breath,
the closer we come to Truth.

50. Ignorance is
    worse than death.
    When our bodies die,
    we learn more about life.
    By pursuing the narrowness of ignorance,
    we grow farther and farther from
    our fellow men.
    Our lives become living death.
    The spiritual awakening of death
    is far sweeter than
    the feeble, groping blindness
    of a life spent in ignorance.

51. To remove
    the blindness of ignorance
    from our eyes,
    we must
    light the lamp
    of Divine Wisdom
    in our hearts.

52. No matter how many times
    you wash a lump of charcoal,
    it will still be black.

53. When will black charcoal
    turn white?
    When you put charcoal into fire,
    it gradually becomes white ashes.
    This is the natural way of things.

54. No matter how many times
    you repeat Jesus' name,
    no matter how long
    you kneel in prayer,
    no matter how much
    you contemplate God's Love,
    the black charcoal
    of your ignorance
    will not turn into
    white spiritual purity,
    without one
    necessary type of
    understanding.
    When you begin to grasp
    the true nature of God
    and His ideal ways on Earth,
    the Light of Divine Wisdom
    will naturally turn every aspect
    of this world
    and the next,
    into bright, glowing whiteness.

There will be no room
for the darkness of ignorance.
Ignoance will disappear automatically.

55.   When Knowledge of God grows,
       ignorance naturally goes.

56.   As long as we allow ourselves
       to be distracted from God
       by worldly affairs
       we will be surrounded
       by ignorance.

57.   If you pick up a matchstick
       which has been soaked in water,
       no matter how many times
       you try to strike it
       against a dry box,
       it will not light.

58.   For a match not to burn
       is bad enough,
       but a wet match
       ruins the box as well.

59.   When your heart is filled
       with cravings for sense pleasures
       and desires for material objects,
       or worldly achievements,
       it is like a water soaked match.

60.   No matter how long
       you strive,
       you will not know
       the glory
       of the knowledge of God,
       if your heart
       is craving the world.

61.   The matchstick
       soaked in water
       is like your heart,
       drenched in desires for
       worldly things,
       and dripping with
       the passions
       of the senses.
       No matter how much you struggle
       trying to do good,
       you will not succeed

until the glory
and warmth
of God's Love
shines in your heart
and dries up the passions
and sense cravings.
Then you will know
the all-embracing comfort
of God's Grace.
You will shine
with the Glory
of God's everlasting Light.

62.   You must live your lives
in spiritual ways.
Spend some time each day
quietly contemplating God.
Dedicate all your actions
to God.
Become worthy of God's Love
and Compassion.
Win God's Grace.

63.   We have seen
a pair of birds
flying together.
The drake is considered
very beautiful to look at.
His companion, the duck,
is drab and not very attractive.
In age after age
throughout Earth's long history,
like this pair of birds,
we see other pairs:
God's Wisdom
and man's ignorance
the eternal and the fleeting,
the non-physical and the physical,
pain and pleasure.
No matter where we see them,
they always exist in pairs.

64.   Like a drake and a duck,
although they appear to be different
neither can exist without the other.
It is the nature of the universe.
It is God's Law.

65.   Trouble and pleasure,
worry and happiness,
cannot exist independently.
Each is half of a pair.
The world is designed in this way.

66. Pleasure and pain
    must exist together.

67. No one can separate them.
    Pleasure and pain
    depend upon each other.

68. You will never find
    happiness on its own,
    anywhere.

69. When pain develops fully
    and ripens,
    it becomes pleasure.

70. We say the
    morning sun
    brings a new day.
    The evening sun
    goes down
    and the day is over.
    Are there two suns —
    one which brings morning light
    and one which precedes darkest night?

71. Just as the same sun
    ushers in both
    lights and darkenss,
    the same mind
    gives us either the lights
    of wisdom
    and spiritual freedom,
    or the darkness
    of ignorance
    and slavery to our senses.
    Our happiness
    and our sorrows
    are products of
    the same mind.

72. O Divine Children of
    the Formless One,
    we must understand this point
    more clearly.
    Let us consider a lock and a key.

73. You put the key
    in the lock.

74. when your turn the key
    to the right,
    the lock opens.

75. When you turn the key
    to the left,
    it locks.

76. For both opening
    or locking,
    we use the same key
    and the same lock.

77. The direction of turning
    causes either locking
    or opening.

78. The sacred consciousness
    in your heart
    is the lock.

79. Your mind
    is the key.

80. When your turn your mind toward
    material gains and worldly cravings,
    your hear will fill up
    with desires,
    worries,
    and frustrations.
    You will be bound
    by your own efforts.
    You will have no peace.
    When you turn your mind
    toward God,
    His Love
    will fill your heart.
    You will know
    the joy of God's Smile.
    You will have infinite
    freedom to do good.

81. Through the ages
    God has sent
    many Spiritual Teachers
    into the world.
    They have shown us
    many avenues to God,
    and given us
    many methods of moving
    along the avenues
    toward God.

82. They have given us
    a great spiritual heritage.
    There are several
    meditative practices.

Among them are the following:
repeating the name of the Lord aloud
or quietly;
contemplating
a Scriptural passage;
contemplating God's Love;
seeing God as our
constant companion
and contemplating
the nature of Divine Light.

They have recommended
kneeling for prayer,
offering incense to God,
and offering
a lighted candle
to God
as altar rites.

We have been given
these types of prayer:
praying to God privately;
praying for the salvation
of the soul;
praying all day
while working;
constant prayer
at all times;
praying during
physical immersion in water;
group prayer;
and prayer to be
filled with the Holy Ghost.
They have suggested
offering thanks to God
for our life and sustenance;
eating blessed food;
admission of personal errors
and attempting to improve;
and serving God
by seeing God
in the husband,
wife and family
as ways
of domestic spiritual life.

Types of group worship include;
reading scriptural passages
and discussing their meanings,
studying the lies of saints,
telling stories of God's glory,

attending religious services,
singing the glories of God
and spreading God's Word.

The essentials of
spiritual community life
are as follows: avoiding bad company,
associating with good people,
being kind to animals,
helping the poor
and suffering,
and extending Divine Love
to all.

They also value
making spiritual pilgrimages
to holy places
and seeking
the blessing of Saints.

They also exemplified
Holy Principles for us
to live by such as the following:
speaking truth;
striving to improve
personal character;
doing good deeds
for their own sake;
dedicating every act
to God;
depending upon God
for all things
and frighting evil forces.

83.   There are many paths
to God's Love.
Whichever path
is you path,
you will eventually reach
the same God.
Each great religious philosophy
had its divine founder.
The founder of each religion
had his particular set of
close disciples.

84.   The three major religious philosophies
of India
are each based on
the ancient Vedic Scriptures 1.

The founder of the philosophy
that "all is One"
— that only God exists
had fourteen major disciples.

85. Four of them held
the most important positions.

86. The Spiritual Teacher
who spread the philosophy
which urges to realize
that we are all God's children,
had six principal followers.

87. The Servant of God
who was sent to proclaim
that we shoudl all act as
God's worthy servants,
had three outstanding devotees.

88. Superior Souls,
who were sent to Earth
with a vision
of the spiritual contribution
that each must make to mankind,
start their respective religions,
spread them
and strengthen them
with the help of a few disciples.

89. Jesus Christ 1
had twelve foremost disciples.

90. Among the twelve
only Judas Simon
would injure Jesus,
their teacher and
spiritual savior.

91. Judas Simon
is well known today
as the disciple
who was treacherous
to his spiritual guide
and guardian.

92. As an important disciple,
Judas was dangerous
because of the greed
in his heart.
Temptation toward money
weakened his judgement.
He promised to deliver Jesus 1
to the priests
somehow or other.

93. Judas
    betrayed God
    for the sake of a mere
    thirty silver coins.

94. Jesus 1 knelt alone in prayer.
    Judas saw Him,
    and stood quietly.
    When Jesus stopped His prayers,
    Judas took His right hand
    and kissed it tenderly.
    He spoke warmly to Jesus
    for some time,
    as would be expected of
    a great devotee.
    Then he took Jesus
    to a lonely place.
    This gave the priests
    the opportunity to be ready.

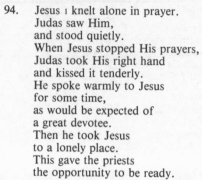

95. As they stood alone,
    the priests came in
    and Judas gave up Jesus 1 to them.

96. From the beginning
    Jesus was a pure, selfless
    a constantly loving person.

97. He unselfishly
    dedicated His every action
    to the good of the world.

98. Early in His life
    He announced,
    "I am God's Messenger 2
    I have come
    as a servant to all God's children."

99. Later He retired
    from the world
    to be alone and contemplate
    the nature of God.
    He was totally immersed in
    the God within Himself
    for twelve years.
    The strength of
    His singular concentration
    drew Him
    much closer to God.

100. By the power of His divine consciousness
      Jesus 1 grew nearer,
      nearer
      and still nearer to God,
      and realized He was Himself
      the Son of God 3.

101. Craving God still more,
      He went on a pilgrimage
      to an isolated part
      of the Himalayan mountains,
      dwelt even more deeply
      and constantly
      in God's Love.
      He continued this practice
      for five years.

102. In his mountain retreat
      He practised a number of
      intense spiritual disciplines.
      He realized
      that the embracing Love
      of the Father
      was His own basic nature.
      He declared,
      "I and My Father
      are One." 4

103. The full awareness of
      His unity with the Almighty
      occured while He was in India.

104. After obtaining Divine Unity
      with God,
      and realizing that He
      and the Holy Ghost
      were One and inseparable;
      He made His way back to
      the countries to the West.
      He has been
      almost completely alone
      for seventeen years.

105. The time had come
      for Him to act
      as an example for others,
      and show them the way to live
      that would bring about
      their salvation.

106. He taught them
      that He was not the only
      Messenger from God 5.

We are all
God's Messengers 5
sent to make a holy mark
in the history of mankind.

107. These Messengers
have become "missing-gers".
Having been sent out by God
to deliver His divine message,
many of us are now missing
from the ranks of the godly.
The missing Messengers
have joined in an unholy campaign
aimed at the destruction of humanity.
Not only have they forgotten
the divine message
in his hearts,
but they are delivering
an opposite message to mankind.

108. The evil ones
of Jesus' 1 time
began torturing Him.
They actually dared to
treat one who had realized Divinity
in that way.

109. Unholy events
happen in every country,
in every world age,
without exception.

110. So it was in Jerusalem.
Judas,
after several attempts,
delivered Jesus
to the priests
who ended His earthly life.

111. By the Grace of God,
the unholiness,
weakness
and doubt
in Judas' heart,
had been partly transformed
by his early exposure to
the Divine Love
of Jesus 1.
Although his burden
of bad qualities was reduced,
Judas was still capable of
wavering in his convictions
and giving in to temptation.

He was also capable
of feeling regret.
His wavering
and lack of self-discipline
eventually cost him his life.
He traded his own life
and the divine life
of Jesus 1, his master,
for a mere thirty coins.
After his treacherous act
he began to think and repent.
"My actions may lead to
the death of my sacred Saviour.
I am the cruellest of the cruel.
I am an unequalled sinner,"
With these thoughts
echoing in his mind.
he hurried to
the great Roman court
where Jesus 1
was being judged guilty
and given the death sentence.
Judas rushed inside,
stood in the courtroom
and said, "These proceedings
are against the law.
I was bribed
by the priests
to give false evidence.
Here are the few coins
they gave me.
Because of the priests,
I told lies.
They are trying to make
the court give wrong judgement.
This is not normal justice.
It is not right."
He said this in a very loud voice
for all to hear.

112.   At that point
the presiding governor
stood up
and said,
"I find him not guilty.
I cannot punish a person
who has committed no crime."

113.   The priests were ready for this.
They had paid
a large group of their followers
to mix with the people
who were watching.

When the court officer
took the case
to the people gathered there,
they bagan shouting,
"Guilty criminal!
Criminal! Criminal!
Jesus 1 is guilty!
Jesus is a criminal!"
The court
took the shouts of the people
who worshipped money
more than God,
as being the decision of the public.
The people
under the priests' control
had done their evil work.

114. Judas saw
that things had gone much further
than he had anticipated.
Feeling all was lost,
he killed himself.

115. The Governor withdrew from
the court.

116. Then the priests banded together
and made their own arrangements
to do away with Jesus 1
the embodiment of compassion.

117. There is no way
for a fully Divine Person
to become angry
or envious,
no matter how many wrongs
are done against them,
or how much trouble
people put them to.

118. The Divine Saviors,
sent by God
to uplift humanity,
are completely
at one with His Divinity.
They know from experience
the true nature of His majesty.

119. They see God clearly
in the three levels
of his own existence.
Their physical bodies
radiate Divine Love.

Their minds
are outpouring rivers
of Divine Love.
They rest always
in the ultimate awareness
of God's infinite expanse
of pure Love.

120. These Great Souls
teach humanity
that each person
is not one person
but three people.

121. The one you think you are.
— You experience yourself as
the body and sense cravings.
The one others think you are.
— They experience you
as your appearence, personality
and mind.
The one you really are.
— God sees you
as an aspect of His own
infinite Divine Consciousness.
This is your true nature.
Over 20,000 years ago
during the time when Rama 6
was the protector of Goodness
in India,
his servant Hanuman 7
was known as someone
who understood fully
the three fold nature
of his own being.

122. So that Hanuman
could share
his insight into reality
with the world,
God spoke as Rama
and asked Hanuman 7
"How do you worship Me?"

123. Hanuman replied,
"When I look at You
from my body,
I am your slave Lord,
and worship You
as my Master.

124. When I look at you
     from my soul,
     You, Lord,
     are the one reality
     and I worship You
     knowing that I am
     Your mirror image.

125. When I look at You
     O Lord,
     from the fullness of my being,
     I can see no begining or end
     between us.

126. You and I are One,
     I am You,
     and You are me.
     We are One dear Lord."

127. God has sent
     Teachers of Divinity to Earth
     since the beginning of time,
     both in India
     and other countries.
     They point the way to
     Salvation,
     and restore Divine Harmony
     on Earth.
     Some of them
     are well known.
     Some are not remembered.
     They each carried out God's plan.

128. In order to honor
     any Divine Teacher
     on His Birthday,
     we must know
     the inner meaning of
     the life He led,
     and the message
     He gave the world.
     Whether it be Jesus 1,
     Rama 2,
     Krishna 3,
     or Sai 4,
     whom we remember,
     we must try to understand
     His message to mankind
     .when we honor Him
     with a Christmas tree
     or other symbol.

129. Today
we think of this day
as Jesus Christ's 1 Birthday.
Its true meaning
is not revealed by luxurious decorations
delicious foods
and the pleasurer of
unending entertainment programs.

130. If we sincerely attempt
to practise the teachings
of a Divine Person,
we can experience
the real meaning
of His Birthday.
Today we waste
this divine opportunity.
We waste the holy Birthday.
We celebrate the day
by doing things
Jesus 1 opposed.
Can unholy actions
create a holy result?

131. Jesus
and His teachings
are not two separatge things.
They are one thing.

132. If we worship
a picture of Jesus 1
but do not pay any attention
to His teachings,
what good does the worship do?
It does no good.

133. Pretending to respect Jesus
but not respecting
His instructions to us,
reduces His status
in the minds of others
and mocks His gift to mankind.

134. A thousand prayers
and no sincere effort
to follow the ways Jesus showed,
do not show
respect for Jesus 1.
Live your life
as Jesus asks;
even if you have no time
for formal worship,
many will benefit.

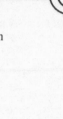

135. Your closeness to God
depends upon how much you value Him
and rely upon Him
in your life.
The quality of your attitude
toward the person in the picture
is what matters.

136. Don't treat
the place where the picture or statue
of Jesus is
as the only holy place
in your home.
Do not worship
God as if He lives in
only a particular picture
or stone sculpture.
God exists everywhere.
Worship Him everywhere.

137. Let the picture of Jesus ı
remind you of God.
Sanctify the picture
by seeing God through it.

138. When you look at
a statue of Jesus,
remember God.
Use the statue
to elevate your view of life.
That is the spirituality
you must bring into being.
That is true worship.

139. When you see the picture,
see God.
Do not see
God as merely a picture.

140. Resolve to remember
God's commands
and attempt to carry them out
whenever you think of the picture.
Let all things
remind you of God.
Try to live as
God wants you to
at all times.
Make this resolution
whole-heartedly and sincerely.

141.   When Westerners see
Eastern people bowing before stones,
they feel amused
and say things like,
"Why do you foolish people
worship stones?"

142.   To understand
the Indian form of worship,
you must realize
that Indians see God
when they look at the stone.
They do not see God
as a piece of stone.

Here are two Indian concepts:
all that exists
is created from the formless God,
and the entirety of existence
is God's divine form.

143.   In India
the awareness
that all is One
is called Non-Dualism 5.

144.   You are
the very Spirit of Divinity.
Regardless of
the shape you consider God to take,
no matter what name
you call Him by,
if you do it
with a pure heart,
a pure concept of God,
and pure Love,
there is every likelihood
that there will be a good result.

145.   Without pure Divine Love
no path
leads to God.
Unselfish Love
is very dear to Him.
His form is Love,
God is Love.

146.   Jesus 1
is the embodiment of
Divine Love.
The path of Divine Love
is the path which leads to Him.

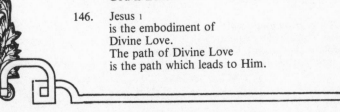

If you wish to reach the top
of a specific mountain
you must climb
that particular mountain.
If you wish to reach
the highest point of perfection
of any quality
you must continually
cultivate that quality.
If you wish to know God's Love,
you must develop
Love of God.

147.   Love is God.
Truth is God.
If you want to know
the truth about God,
you must follow
the path of Truth.
Only the path of Love
leads to God's Love.

148.   If you want to see
the cool, white moon
on a dark night,
will a torch
or a spotlight
help you see the moon
more clearly?

149.   The moon
is made visible
by the light reflected
by the moon.

150.   You may say,
"I want Jesus 1.
I want to see Jesus.
I want to feel Jesus."
Jesus
is the embodiment of
Divine Love.
If you fill your heart
with Divine Love,
then you will experience Jesus
who is Love.
There is no other way.

151.   If you truly long to see
the Truth of His Divinity,
follow the path of Truth very closely
until you see Him.

152. Seeing you as Love,
I must tell you this.
Whenever there is a person
who is of high spiritual value
to mankind,
there are people
filled with wickedness,
who follow Him
wherever He goes.
These wicked people
torment Him
and give Him endless trouble.
This happened in Jesus' day.
It happens today,
and it will happen
in every future age.

153. Consider a diamond.
It has been scratched,
chiselled and broken
many times
in order to expose its many faces
to the sunlight,
so that we may admire
its brilliant sparkle.
The better it is cut,
the more its value is increased.

154. If a rough diamond
is displayed
in its natural state,
people may look at it with curiosity,
but they say,
"It is an uncut stone.
Who knows
what it's really worth?"

155. In the case of gold,
you may find a small bag
of gold nuggets
in an old trunk.
Someone may offer you
a certain price.
If you have
the gold nuggets cleaned,
separate the impurities with fire,
and hammer the shaped
the purified gold into rings;
its value will be much higher.

156. The Divine Messengers
God sends to Earth
are like precious gold
and diamonds.
The more they are troubled,
tested,
accused
and attacked,
the more their spiritual fame
spreads in the world.
The trials they face
can never reduce
their true Divinity.

157. The more the evil-minded father
of the young boy, Pralad
attacked him,
and tried to distract him
from God,
the more Pralad 6
called upon God
for salvation,
and the more devoted to God
he became.

158. Once long ago
there was a godly king
who was known for his honesty.
Sage Vishwamitra 7
who was known for his violent temper,
decided to test the king.
By various means
he stripped the king of his kingdom,
wealth,
loyal wife
and son.
No matter what happened,
King Hari 8 remained **truthful**
and **true to his word.**
His fame grew tremendously
because of his uncompromising
adherence to Truth.
Because of the extreme trials
he underwent,
he is still famous throughout India
as an upholder of Truth.
Mahatma Gandhi
was inspired by his story
and modelled his own life
along truthful lines.

So one could say
that present day India
owes its freedom
not only to King Hari's [8] example,
but to Vishwamitra [7]
who severly tested him.
Adversaries are very valuable
to future generations.

159. Jesus [1] was tortured
by the Jewish priests and villains.
The more He was tortured,
the more famous
He became.
Torturing and **temptation**
improve the reputation
of great Souls.

160. The Divine Incarnations [9]
are not harmed in any way
by the challenges
and tortures They undergo.
Those devoted to
the path of the tortured one
may temporarily lose
their peace of mind.

161. We look at a ring
on a finger and think
it is a **very simple thing.**

162. We forget
the gold-mining,
the heat of the smelting,
the hammering,
filing and polishing
that go into the making of
that simple ring.

163. Please realize
that when followers of
our Indian spiritual traditions
are suppressed,
troubled,
and given countless sorrow,
and harsh treatment,
they are forced to concentrate
much more strongly on
pure, formless God.

164. These stresses
will not be difficult to bear
if we see them
as the passing clouds
they really are.
They are not lasting things.

165. Embodiments of Divine Love, ·
our human life has limits.

166. Pulse and blood pressure
have **limits.**

167. The human eye can see only
certain types of light
within a narrow range of brightness.

168. Blood must circulate
inside the blood vessels.
Blood flowing outside the vessels
is dangerous.

169. Our bodies suffer
if we eat more than
or less than certain amounts.

170. Too much sound
breaks our ear drums.

171. Our earthly life itself
is a short-term opportunity.

172. Yet we try one thing after another
to keep our bodies
alive for ever.
This is foolishness.
Life lasts as long as God wills.
Earth life ends when God
takes us away from the body.
As long as we are alive on earth,
it is our duty to dedicate our energies
to the unselfish service of others.
To do this,
we must keep our consciousness
and mind
pure and loving.

173. You must manifest
the Love of God
in your life.
Unselfish service is God.
Whenever you have the opportunity,
do your best to serve unselfishly.

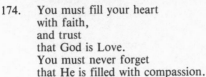

Peaceful, heart-warming
conversation about God
with people of good character,
is of great value.

174. You must fill your heart
with faith,
and trust
that God is Love.
You must never forget
that He is filled with compassion.

175. Don't go through life thinking,
"God is troubling me.
God is testing me.
God is angry with me."
That is imagination.
It is pure illusion.

176. Whether we are aware of it or not,
our very action
causes a reaction —
our own actions
create the pain
or pleasure we experience.
No one else gives it to us.

177. When we do good,
good comes our way.

178. There is a right way to live.
Develop good thoughts.
Always be ready to do good.
Constantly do good deeds.

"Follow Jesus" Index.

1979

CHRISTMAS DISCOURSE

1. There are those who say,
   "Vishnu 1 is the preserver of creation.
   All should worship Him,"
   while some othes believe,
   "Shiva 2, the destroyer of evil,
   rules all destiny.
   Truly He deserves all praise."

   Others glorify Ganesha 3
   saying, "He alone is with us
   in times of need.
   Pray to Him."

   Scholars devoted to learning,
   declare, "Truth alone
   is the greatest God.
   We dedicate our lives to
   Wisdom."

   Still others,
   fervent followers of Muhammad4,
   proclaim, "God's name is Allah.
   There is no other to surrender to."

   And faithful Christians 5 say,
   "Christ alone is the way.
   In his name
   we pray."

   My devotees regard
   Sai 6 as Divinity,
   and they look on Me.
   Everyone should realize
   that truly
   all are One.

   What then
   of this seeming diversity?
   When we look carefully
   into the devoted heart,
   we see
   that whatever the chosen faith may be,
   all agree
   that the way of Love
   is the path to God.

   This is the Truth of truths.
   The purest Love
   is the highest path
   for everyone.

2. There are many ways
to express love.

Those who view the world
with pure love,
find love in all they view.
Seeing all as good,
seeing nothing as bad,
many people — simple,
good natured,
gentle people —
encourage love
in everything
and everyone
they see.

There are some others
who turn their love
toward education,
and claiming wisdo9m
say,
"Right is right,
and wrong
is wrong."

As well as these,
there are also
some bad people
who ignore
all
right
and point
a critical finger
at the wrong,
because they love to argue
and fight.

There are some evil people
who love darkness
far more than lights.
They use force
to make all right things
into wrong things.
The good natured,
the educated
and the argumentative
form the better group.
But even a person
who is possessed
by the demonic,
is better than someone
who forces right people
into the wrong.

131

These four types of people
played roles
in the life of Christ. 1

3.   Though Christian 2 ways
have nearly been forgotten,
money is remembered
every moment of the day.

No baby brings
gold coins with him
from his mother's womb.

Your money won't follow you
into the next world
when your time has come.

Even a millionaire
has to live
on simple starch
and protein.
Even his stomach
cannot digest
pure
glittering gold.

Though you may be
very proud
about becoming
rich,
will money follow you
beyond the grave?
Will it go
to thieves?
Will it be taken
as taxes?

The blossoms
and trees
obey the Lord on high.
Don't sweet smelling flowers
give their nectar freely
to every passing bee?
Don't fruit tree
feed all
who pass their way?

What more
can I say to you
than this?

4.   Embodiments
of Divine Love!

Modern man
has gone
off the right path.
The Love, Truth, and Purity
of Jesus 1 have been forgotten.
Today's man
is pursuing
unrestrained
cravings
for worldly objects
and physical sensations.

5. There is no limit
to his cravings.

6. Man,
trapped in the web
of his desires,
is suffering.

7. No matter how much
name,
fame,
wealth,
property
and power
a man has,
he is never satisfied.
His mind churns endlessly
trying to derive
spiritual peace
from physical objects.

8. By constantly collecting
new and better worldly possessions,
he wastes precious time
in the hope
of achieving satisfaction.
There is no
material object in creation
that will give mental comfort,
and grant everlasting peace.

9. Unfit pursuits
not only
waste time,
they drag
man's mind
to a low level.
Love for the physical
is misplaced.
Constantly chasing
physical love
and objects of desire

is a misuse
of your divine human life.

10. There is a vast difference
between what we see as valuable
and what is truly valuable.
In this world
the true wealth
is the wealth
of contentment.

11. A greedy man
is a most unfortunate
person.
Of all humans,
he is the most
miserable person
in the world.
The difference
between the things we give
our attention to
and the things which
truly deserve our attention
is a measure
of our personal greed and ignorance.
Following the dictates of greed
can never reward us
with true satisfaction
or mental comfort.

12. Who is the
poorest man
in the world?
He
who has
the most desires.
Who is
the richest man
He who is
most satisfied.

13. A person's health,
a person's happiness,
a person's comfort,
all interpersonal relationships —
the totality of
a man's well being,
depends upon
his degree of
contentment.

14. Worry, sorrow,
discord, strife, stress
and emotionalism
destroy the
fruits of a man's
labor and ultimately may rob
him of life itself.
Only after
we have developed
the good quality
of contentment
is it possible
to purify
human life, and attain
the goal of human life
which is Divinity.

15. You may be rich.

16. You may be very intelligent.

17. You may be
in a very powerful
position.

18. But,
if you do not have a tender heart
that is larger than
your position of power,
your wealth,
and intelligence,
all this status is useless.
You have the power to create,
but you do not have
the kindness and compassion
to help even yourself.

19. When a person
embraces morality,
radiates spirituality,
and does truly good things,
he shines
with the brilliance
of his true Divinity.

20. If a man spends
all day,
every day,
pursuing
worldly
and material goals,

this short,
sacred,
human life
will be thrown away
uselessly.

21. History is filled with
     examples
     of the weakness of the physical,
     and the infinite strength
     of Divinity.
     Long ago
     Vishwamitra 1
     ruled
     in India.
     He became obsessed
     by his own strength
     and mental powers.
     He attacked
     a God-filled sage
     called Vasishta. 2
     Time and again
     he attacked;
     Time and again
     he and his armies
     were totally
     put to shame.
     They were unable to withstand
     the power of God
     which was at Vasishta's command.

22. Eventually
     King Vishwamitra
     realized that
     physical
     and mental powers
     are merely
     the shadow
     of the Power
     of the Creator.
     Vishwamitra 1 began
     to concentrate on God.
     He took up spiritual practices,
     and after years of dedication
     to Divinity,
     he overcame anger
     and he himself became divine.

23. More recently,
    one hundred members
    of the ruling
    Kaurava Dynasty 2
    became intoxicated
    by wealth
    and military
    might.
    They nursed a grudge
    against the five
    God-following
    Pandava brothers. 3

24. During a tremendous battle,
    the Kauravas
    were killed
    to the last man.
    Vast numbers
    and sheer force of arms
    will always fail
    before the power God gives to
    the truly faithful few.

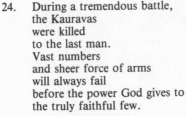

25. In another period,
    just as today's scientists
    are proud of their attempts
    to conquer outer space,
    the two wicked Gold brothers 2,
    became proud of
    their personal mastery
    of the elements of nature.
    In their arrogance
    they began playing
    havoc with all humanity.

26. When men
    who cannot control
    their own
    internal lust,
    anger,
    hatred,
    jealousy,
    and sense cravings,
    attempt to master
    the external
    elements of nature,
    they will ultimately
    accomplish nothing.

27. We must first
gain control
of our senses
and master
the internal sphere
of our emotions.
Only then
will we be able to obtain
external happiness
and enjoy
the contentment of
internal
Divine Peace.

28. Every living being
in this world
is knowingly or unknowingly
on a spiritual pilgrimage.

29. In your life's pilgrimage
where
is destiny leading you?

30. According to
the "Book of God's Love,"
the Bhagavatha,
"it is the nature of all beings
to return to the place
where they were
originally created."

31. The crucial quesion is,
"Where has life come from?"

32. God
answers this question
in his
"Song of God,"
"the bhagavad Geeta." [1]
God says,
"From the beginning of time,
all beings
have come into this world
from My Own
Infinite Being.

33. This universe,
the heavens,
the lower world and all beings —

— The entire
infinite life form
is emerging from
Me,
with My Own qualities
hidden in it.''

34.   So
the destination of
your life's pilgrimage
and that of all beings,
is a conscious reunion
with the same God
from which
you have come.

35.   There is no avoiding it,
every being
will reach
his place
of spiritual origin.

36.   Here is an example;
water is like consciousness.
the sun shines
on the surface
of the ocean,
ocean water evaporates
and rises into the clouds,
the evaporated ocean water
falls as rain
and rivers form;
the rivers finally merge into
the very same ocean.
Man's consciousness,
like river water,
moves with great speed and force
in the direction of its origin!
The river
moves towards the sea,
man's consciousness
moves towards God.

37.   It is essential
that man
follows closely
the example
set by the rivers.

38.   Humans who display their
best nature
bear patiently
all the difficulties,

sorrows,
and losses
along their path
to God.
They do not let
obstacles divert their concentration
from God.
Their consciousness
moves very fast
toward God Realization.

39. Every man
     is the
     embodiment of God.

40. Man has come
     into this world
     as a Messenger
     from God. 1
     His purpose here
     is to recognize
     and realize
     his own
     God given destiny.

41. Recognizing this Truth,
     Jesus Christ 2
     initially announced,
     "I am a Messenger
     sent from God."

42. God's Messenger,
     Jesus,
     spent many years practising spiritual austerities,
     so that
     He woud be able to
     shower compassion
     and Divine Love
     on all humanity.

43. Then He asked Himself,
     "Am I part of God
     or am I just
     something related to God?"

44. He spent twelve years
     wandering alone
     in deserts,
     considering this point.

45. Then He returned to
     society
     and proclaimed,
     "I am
     the Son of God." 1

46. While saying this,
    He dedicated His life
    entirely to
    the uplift
    of society
    with great compassion
    and love.

47. Due to the efforts
    of selfish,
    egoistic men,
    who dedicated
    their lives
    to atrocities
    and lawbreaking,
    evil crept
    into the holy temples
    in Jerusalem.
    Businesses
    and impure practices
    sprang up.

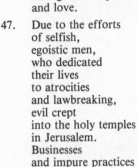

48. Seeing these evils,
    Jesus 2 tried repeatedly
    to drive out
    the corruption.

49. It was at this point
    that Jesus 2
    reached the stage described
    in the Indian
    guide books to right living,
    the Shastras,
    where He realized,
    "All forms
    are God's own Divine Form."

    Accordingly,
    when He was asked
    "Who are you?",
    Jesus answered,
    "I and My Father
    are One." 3

50. Jesus tried to
    show every human
    the Fatherhood of God
    and the Brotherhood
    of Man.

51. A percentage of the people
     did not believe Jesus,
     considered Him a false prophet,
     and tried
     to thwart His mission.

52. Faced with countless
     trials,
     tribulations
     and upsets,
     Jesus chose to
     continue being
     an example of
     living Truth
     and carried on with
     his preaching mission.

53. Completely unconcerned
     about the physical conditions
     He had to undergo,
     He put the
     purity of society
     first
     and proclaimed Divine Purity
     to the world,
     despite all obstacles.

54. During this period
     Jesus had disciples
     who followed Him.

55. Throughout history,
     whether it be
     Jesus' 1 time,
     Muhammad's 2 time,
     Rama's 3 time,
     Krishna's 4 time,
     or any other time,
     followers have never
     at any time
     had full,
     stable,
     strong
     and unwavering
     devotion.

56. Followers may believe
     that they are devotees
     or disciples,
     but in truth
     they are not fully devoted.

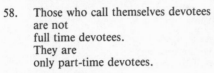

57. As long as devotees
    are happy
    they follow their master
    very closely,
    but
    when trouble arises,
    they go their own ways.

58. Those who call themselves devotees
    are not
    full time devotees.
    They are
    only part-time devotees.

59. Jesus had twelve
    main disciples.

60. Most of them loved Jesus,
    followed His ideals,
    and put them
    into practice.

61. This world
    is filled with greed
    for money.

62. For a long time
    man has been possessed
    by his idea that money
    is more important
    than character,
    that this world runs on money,
    that money alone is important.

63. Some people became jealous
    of Jesus' 1 growing popularity
    and fame.
    Provoked by priests,
    they tried to bribe His disciple
    Judas.

64. When he saw the money,
    Judas lost control:
    greed
    possessed him.
    Although
    he should have
    lived as if Jesus
    were his very life,
    Judas sold Jesus
    to the priests
    for a mere thirty coins.

65. Because he sold
     his master's life
     for money,
     he could not
     enjoy his own life.
     His mind
     gave him no peace.
     Finally he gave up
     and committed suicide.

66. This type of thing
     has not been happening
     for the last 2000 years,
     or the last 5000 years,
     or for the last 100,000 years.
     From the very beginning of time
     the same pattern has occurred.
     Corrupt, greedy.
     selfish people
     dishonor their spiritual teachers
     by spreading
     false rumors about them.

67. Actually
     the number of Judases
     on earth
     was very small
     2000 years ago.

68. According to an Eastern tradition
     time is divided into various ages.
     This current age
     started above five thousand years ago.
     The outstanding characteristics
     of this age
     are deceit, rivalry
     and quarrelling.
     Thus it is called the Kali Age
     or the age of quarrelling.
     In the Kali Age
     people
     obsessed with money
     spread false impressions
     about the very same
     spiritual teachers
     whom they should love
     as much as they love
     life.
     This is a great sin!

69. What is real wealth today?

70. Some think of buildings
and land
as truly valuable.

71. Or gold and silver
may be cherished.

72. Paper money and dollars
may be hoarded.

73. None of these is
true wealth.

74. Good character
is true wealth.

75. Good conduct
should be seen
as true wealth.
Wisdom is wealth.

76. To have the wisdom
of the Most High
is to possess God.

77. Your true wealth
is your good character,
your good conduct
and your knowledge of God.

78. Today
we have lost
these three sacred treasures.
Today we dedicate our lives
to the unreal,
the temporary,
world wealth.

79. How long
will your worldly possessions
be near you?
As long as
your worldly body lasts.

80. When we give up this body
we also give up gold,
silver,
cars,
and all material objects.

81. But the wealth
of Divine Wisdom
is different.

82. The Divine Wisdom you gain
will be in you,
move with you,
and stay with you,
and protect you,
as the eyelid
protects the eye.
It will beckon you
and lighten your entire path
to complete Union
with the Inifinite.

83. Strive to acquire
the wealth of wisdom.
Then
in the light of your wisdom,
examine the true nature
of both the physical
and the spiritual.
Try to see the Truth
common to
both types of wealth.
Find ways that your wealth
can best serve humanity
and God.
What good
is Divine Knowledge
if it is not used
to bring us closer to God?

84. Today's man
pretends he knows everything.

85. He knows many things about
current events in America,
Russia
and England.
He knows about astronomy
and about the Earth.

86. But he does not know
who
he truly is.

87. All knowledge is useless to
a person
who does not know
his own
true nature.

88. From the moment
he gets up in the morning

and throughout
every minute of the day
man says,
"my".

89. My house,
my body,
my car,
my school;
all
my, my, my.
But who is this
"my"?
Who am "I"?
He never asks that question!

90. Trapped in his body
he suffers countless miseries.

91. When you think
"This is my body",
it is obvious that
you are not the body.

92. "This is my handkerchief"
means
I am not this handkerchief.

93. You must see that
this "you"
whom you call "I"
exists
on a separate plane.

94. Knowledge
can never be complete
until you know
the secret of the self.

95. Even though you may count
all the stars in the sky
and walk on the moon,
you are walking away from
any hope
of Bliss
if you do not know
who you truly are.

96. You live in the body,
you are not the body.

97. You are the farmer,
the body and senses
are the field.

98. A man
encourages the growth of
many different things
in his body,
his field.
He cultivates
numerous sense cravings:
Beneficial fruits
are not produced by
a field of weeds.

99. But if you sow the seeds
of good deeds,
then you will reap the harvest
of happiness.

100. When you sow the seeds
of evil acts,
you surround yourself
with sorrow and grief.

101. Thus every step of the way
you are responsible
for creating
your own happiness
and suffering —
not God!

102. Today's man
blames God
for all the good and bad
that befalls him.
Man alone
is the source
of his own misery
or his happiness.

103. This physical world
is not the highest reality.
In fact
it is unreal.
This world is the
world of humans,
who will one day
cease to be.
All that we see or sense
is impermanent.
It is only temporary
physical reality.

Because we cling
to the impermanent
we become unhappy.

That which is truly real
does not change.
Divine reality
is permanent.

104. This world has
two important qualities.

105. This world
is not permanent.
This world
is full of unhappiness, sorrow,
displeasure.

106. Knowing worldly life
is not permanent,
pray to God
for everlasting bliss.
The two important characteristics
of this world
are
that it is filled with misery
and that it won't last.

107. Not one thing
in this world is
permanent.

108. Each thing
is ever changing.
Nothing here is eternal.

109. For all things
which come together
and unite,
coming apart
is unavoidable.

110. Today's man wants everything to
come together
and nothing
to fall apart.

111. "One way traffic"
is not possible
in this world.

112. Within the realm
of man's physical experience
all things which join together
must one day
move apart.
In a world full of change,
people constantly
attempt to create
unchanging physical circumstances.

They experience
feelings of mental insecurity
and emotional unrest
when unwanted changes occur.

They mourn
and grieve over separation.
In a world of constant change,
continuous expansion
and contraction,
endless separations
and reunions must occur.
If we emotionally demand
constant physical stability
will we ever be happy?

113.   Being content
to let go of things
is the only guarantee
of peace
and happiness
for humanity.

114.   For example:

115.   The wool coat
that you hold close to you
to keep warm with in winter,
is useless in summer.
So
you hang it in the closet.

116.   But thin summer clothes
are put away in winter.

117.   This separation
has nothing to do with
how much you like the
clothing.
It depends upon
the outside temperature.

118.   Your wool coat
warms your body
in winter.

119   Timeless
Truth
warms your heart
the whole year through.

120.   Physical objects
offer only
limited usefulness;
infinite Truth gives infinite service.

121. Here is another example:

122. We inhale air.

123. If we do not
      breathe out
      the air we inhale
      our lungs will be damaged.

124. We take in food.
      If the food
      does not pass
      out of the body,
      the digestive organs
      will be damaged.

125. Similarly,
      if circulating blood
      does not leave the place
      where it was a moment ago,
      swelling will occur.

126. Coming together
      and separating
      is the very nature of things.
      Our hopes and happiness
      should not depend upon
      the presence or absence.

127. We all agree
      that each man
      has some good traits
      and some
      bad traits.
      Calmness
      and good judgement
      are necessary
      for our spiritual progress.

128. Knowing this
      we should
      look with an equal eye
      and maintain a calm mind
      during both praise
      and blame.

129. That is true
      self control.

130. Only the day
      that we achieve
      true self control
      will we also achieve
      true Divinity.

131. Feeling elated about praise
and depressed
about blame
is not man's
true nature.

132. You must attain
equal-mindedness.
Equanimity
is called "yoga".
All things bring peace
when the mind is
all Love.

133. With equal-mindedness
and abundant Love,
we can become
talented in handling
both spiritual
and worldly matters.

134. To improve our talents
we must improve our knowledge
of the higher planes of existene:
the Divine Planes.

135. First
we must gain
Divine Knowledge.

136. In our attempts
to apply Divine Knowledge
we develop skill.

137. Thirdly
comes emotional balance
and good natured self-discipline.

138. The Soul
becomes a haven of peace.
In this atmosphere
insight arises.

139. Balance
comes from
skillful use of
Divine Knowledge.

140. Today
instead of skillfully developing
your Divine Knowledge
you are killing
your Divinity.

141. When you kill
Divine Knowledge
you have no steadiness.
You lose your balance.

142. Today
man grossly misuses
his precious knowledge.

143. Man follows many
wrong paths.

144. He applies his knowledge
to develop
temporary life styles,
based on
useless over-consumption
in the world
he may have to leave tomorrow.

145. Using fragrant sandal wood
as firewood
is wrong.
Its sweet smelling oil
should be used
to make incense
which may be offered
to the Lord.

146. We are using diamonds
as.charcoal.

147. we exchange
precious human life
for useless notoriety
and infamy.

148. This body is like
a traveler's overnight
rest-house.

149 It is like
a hotel
for the Soul.
As such
it is a temporary
resting place.

150. Like a watchman
for the hotel,
the mind
is a watchman
for the body.

151. Life-force or Soul
is the traveler
on a holy journey.

152. There is no lasting
connection between
the traveler,
the watchman
and the hotel.

153. Their relationship
is only temporary
and fleeting.
You are not
permanentaly attached to
your mind.
Nor do you own the body.

154. We should not waste
this divine human life.

155. This body is lifeless
and negative in nature.
It's not alive.

156. When there is a divine positive
living within,
this negative body
can be put to good use.

157. We make no attempt
to live in harmony with
our true infinite nature
which is the source
of the mind.
We ignore
our own
innate Divinity.
Yet
we strive ceaselessly
to fulfill
every negative need
of this lifeless body.

158. When will your body
be filled
with
the Holy Spirit?

159. When you yourself
become
infinite,
all-embracing
Love.

160. Without
all-embracing
Divine Love,
your life
is living death.

161. When you are
Divine Love,
all creation
is in your hands.

162. Jesus 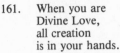 1 was a person
whose only joy
was spreading Divine Love,
offering Divine Love,
receiving Divine Love,
living as
Divine Love.

163. Many accused Jesus
of being a false prophet.
He had to live under
constant attack.

164. Some say
Jesus was born on
December, twenty-fifth.

165. David Hedge,
the English astronomer,
calculated that Jesus 1
was born
on September fifteenth.

166. His September 15th. figure
was based on
limited information.

167. Once every 800 years
a certain
bright star appears.

168. The Bible says
Jesus' Birth Day
was heralded by
a bright tar.

169. Based on these facts
the astronomer announced
that Jesus was born
only 800
years ago.

170. 800 years ago!

171. This is not true.

172. Jesus was born
early in the morning
at 3:15 a.m.
on December 24th.
one thousand
nine hundred and eighty
years ago.

173. It was Sunday.

174. His Divine Body
grew up in the world.

175. The bright star
that appeared
on His Birthday
was the same bright star
which appears
once every 800 years.

176. The bright star appeared
because of its own
natural pattern,
not because of Jesus.

177. Emotional people say
this star appeared for Jesus. [1]

178. There is no rule
that bright stars
must appear
when divine energies
or Divine Incarnations [2]
descend to earth.

179. In their emotion
about God
devotees spread sentimental stories.

180. Jesus Himself
is a star
of infinite value.

181. He Himself
spreads a great brilliance.

182. Must His brilliance
be accompanied by
another glow?

183. We go along with these things
to keep devotees happy.

184. Today is Jesus' Birthday.
It is useless to put up lights
and Christmas trees
amidst winter snowfalls
in December,
even if we pray
the whole day through.
It is useless to pray for one day
and forget about God
all the rest of the year.

185. It is not a show of Love
arising from the Heart.
It is just an
empty show.

186. When we live and practice
Jesus' 1 teachings,
we are true Christians, 2
not before.

187. If we actually followed
only two statements
Jesus made,
that would be enough.

188. Instead we develop prejudice
and narrow-mindednes.
If we truly follow
"All life is One,
My Dear Son.
Be alike
to everyone", 3
that is enough.

189. "All life is One
My dear Son.
Be alike
to everyone."

190. Are we following it?

191. If we are not,
what is the use of
celebrating
Jesus' 1 Birthday?

192. We say we want Jesus.
But we ignore His commands.
Of what use
are such prayers?

193. Even if you do not celebrate His Birthday,
it does not make any difference.
Follow Him!

That is enough!
Follow!

194. Jesus showed us
many ideal ways
for a human to live.
He set
a living example.

195. When He was crucified,
many of His flock
were overcome
with agony.

196. Then an unknown voice
from the heavens
said
"Death
is the dress
of life".

197. Just as we put clothes
on the body,
the body itself
is the clothing
of the Divine Spirit.

198. When we send this robe
out to the laundry
do we cry?

199. Do **you** cry?

200. Does anyone cry
when this robe gets old
and worn out?

201. When a body falls away,
no one should cry.

202. Burning is the nature of fire.

203. Coolness
is natural to water.

204 Death
is natural
to a body.

205. Fire is hot.
Is anyone
surprised?

206. We should not be surprised
in the slightest
when the body
fades away.

207. That which causes birth
also causes death.

208. We search endlessly
looking for causes
of physical death.
But no one looks
for the divine source
of life.

209. Such research
is a waste of time.
It is better
not to search for either cause,
than to conduct
purely physical investigations.

210. Glorify your brief span
between birth and death.
Do God's work!

211. Divine Incarnations, 4
ideals for humanity,
have come to Earth;
not only in Western countries
but also in India.
They gave their lives
to uplift humanity.

212. People
consider each man different,
but God is One.

213. Our bodies may look different,
our life styles may differ,
when and where
we are born may be different,
our spoken languages
may be different,
but the Spirit of Love
in all of our religions
is one and the same.

214. When and where we were born
influences the way
we worship.
But our true religion,
Divine Love,
is one and the same.

215. We use many languages
on Earth;
the language of Love
in our hearts
is one and the same.

216. There is only one God.
He is present everywhere.

217. There is only one race —
the race of mankind

218. There is only one religion —
the religion of Love.

219. There is only one language —
the language of the heart.

220. The true meaning of human life
can be known
when we embrace
the living spirit of those four.

Which country does not matter,
your generation does not matter,
no physical condition matters.
Living life
with your hearts
overflowing with Love,
making your every act sacred,
does matter.

221. We enshrine petty differences
of nationality,
language,
race
and religion.
We kill
the love in our hearts.

222. We should honor
and nurture
the love in our hearts,
keep the ideals
of Jesus [1]
ever in view,
become living examples
of Love,
and experience
the spirit of Jesus
as our personal Messenger [2]
sent from God.

223. Love alone
let you see
the true Divinity.

224. Love is essential.
"God is Love".
Live in Love.

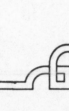

225. Love lives by giving
and forgiving.

226. Self lives by getting
and forgetting.

227. Love is selflessness.
Selfishness is lovelessness.

228. We should not worship narrow
self-interest.
We should
Love — Love — Love.

229. Tread the Path
of Love.
Become the Ultimate You,
what you truly are.
Become the living embodiment
of Love.

230. No matter what others
think about you,
no matter how they
treat you,
don't worry
in the least.
Follow the Divine Person.
Follow Jesus Christ. 1

231. Live
for your own evolution.
Do not live for
what others will say.

232. You have your own life,
your own heart,
your own opinion,
your own ideas
and your own will.

233. There is no need for you
to imitate others.

234. Imitation is human.
Creation is divine.

235. Follow your own path.
Let your own experience of God
be your master.

236. Follow the Master.

237. Face the Devil,
temptation.

238. Fight to the end.

239. Finish the game.

240. Carry out thse four.
Don't go to your grave
weakly copying
other people.

241. Conduct research.
Find your sacred spirit.

242. You won't find God
in the outside world.

243. Your own loving heart
is God's home.

244. You are God.
The true you
is God.

245. You are not one person.

246. But three.

247. The one you think
you are.

248. The one others think
you are.

249. And the one
you really are.

250. You assume three forms
You think of yoruself
as your body
and sense cravings.
Others
think you are
your personality,
and appearance.
You truly are
Infinite Spirit.

251. Because we **are**
Infinite Spirit
we should constantly
remind ourselves,
"I am God,
I am God,
I am God!"

252. The day you truly
see yourself
as God,
you become God.

253. The infinite
Divine Spirit
takes over.

254. Thinking,
"I am human,
I am human,"
leads you astray.

255. Your body
is a human body,
but your spirit
is the living spirit of God.

256. Do not let your body
dictate your every move.

257. Let God lead you.

258. Do not
over-emphasize
outside vision.
Develop
inner vision.

259. Then you will
become
Man Divine.

260. The body is a cart.

261. The spirit
you are,
is like a horse.

262. Put the horse before the cart.
Let the spirit guide
the body.

263. Nowadays
no one does this.

264. Body,
body,
body.
Body comfort,
body happiness;
sense pleasure —
we think of nothing else.

265. With the cart before the horse,
it is impossible
to get anywhere.

266. Infinite,
divine,
spiritual peace of mind
is important.

267. What you do
with your mind
enslaves your Soul
or liberates you.

268. All the luxury in the world
cannot give peace of mind.

What good is body comfort
if you are unhappy?

269. The body
is well dressed.

270. The dining-room chairs
have padded seats.

271. The house
is air-conditioned.

272. The room
is filled with cool air,
but our minds
are full of hot air,
burning with desire.

273. Is
the mind air-conditioned?

274. All this cools the body,
but overheats
the mind.

275. How vital
is physical comfort
in life?

276. Mental comfort
is important,
not physical comfort.

277. Take up spiritual practice.
Spiritual practice
is the only route
to "mental comfort",
true peace of mind.
There is no other path

278. Everyone knows
that the average American
is materially
very well off.
Rich men are very common.

279. There are large cars everywhere.

280. If we placed
all the cars
in the United States of America
end to end,
they would literally
reach the moon.

281. But there is no
true happiness.

282. No
divine bliss.

283. No
peace of mind.

284. Money
cannot buy
peace of mind.
Power
cannot command
peace of mind.
Virtue alone
guarantees
blessed peace.

285. Are you ready
for the Grace
of God?
Cultivate divine virtues;
preserve
and protect
good qualities.
Realize their sacredness.
Then alone
will you be fit
for God's Grace.

286. Embodiments of infinite Love,
listen!
Every material thing
in this world
has to be left behind.
It is
a passing cloud.

287. Here nothing is permanent.

288. Why trade permanent
      peace of mind
      for impermanent
      physical luxuries?

289. Every word we say
      should be divine.

290. You may not be able
      to oblige or agree,
      but you can always
      speak
      obligingly,
      pleasantly.

291. Try to speak sweetly.

292. Give comfort with
      your every glance.

293. Divine conduct
      is a must.

294. Mold your self-discipline,
      your habits,
      into a divine pattern.
      Everything around you
      must take
      a divine shape.

295. Let your
      divine life style
      be a fit example
      for others.

296. Don't live
      like an animal,
      a slave
      to your sense pleasures.

297. Don't be a puppet
      in the hands
      of sense gratification.

298. Once long ago,
      a small boy
      named Pralad ₁
      spoke to his father.

299. "O father,
      with great ease
      you have conquered the heavens,
      the Earth, and the underworld.

But you forgot
the world of
lust and desire.
You forgot
to conquer
your mind."

300. Vanquishing
the external world
is useless.

301. Conquer lust.
Vanquish anger.
Exile greed,
hate,
and jealousy.

302. Dedicate
all your God-given senses
to winning
God's grace.

303. Rise above
your physical fancies.

Don't allow them
to make you
act like
an animal.

304. By chasing
worldly sense cravings,
all of which
are short lived,
your plight
has become
worse
than an animals'.

305. Quite frankly
the behaviour
of jungle animals
is better.

306. Wild animals
act out of need
and only
in season.

307. Man
acts
for no reason.
He moves
out of season.

308. Obviously
so-called "wild"
animals
are behaving
better than
so-called
humans.

309. Dedicate
your hands
to the service of
mankind!

310. Hands
in society,
head
in the cool,
peaceful forest.

311. That way
you will have
a peaceful life.

312. Jesus  renounced everything
to become
fit for
service to mankind.

313. Jesus
teaches Divine Love
and infinite compassion.
Without these
man
is in no way
human.

314. To resurrect
love
and compassion,
we must
kill jealousy
and selfishness.

315. We are murdering
our heart's
true children.
We have forgotten
how to cultivate
true
Divine Love.
But we are accomplished masters
of selfish greed.

We are trained professionals
at saving time,
at the expense of
genuine acts of kindness.
We allow
hidden, jealous rage
to motivate
our every move.
Love
and compassion
are being choked to death
by the grasping hands
of our own selfish greed.

316. I anticipate
that you will
develop compassion
and Love,
purify your hearts,
and leave
a sacred legacy
to future generations,
earn the true mercy
of Jesus, 1
follow the path
shown by Him
and reach the position
He holds.

Expecting you to do this
I conclude
this discourse.

GLOSSARY INDEX

ISLAM

THE RELIGION OF MUHAMMAD —

1. According to the Old Testament the Lord spoke to Abraham, the father of Isaac, about his eldest son by his Egyptian wife Hagar.

God said, "I will bless your son Ishmael and multiply him exceedingly. I will make a great nation of his descendants." Gen. 17-20

2. In the sixth century after Jesus Christ's birth, a prophet was born among the descendants of Ishmael, the son of Abraham. His name was Muhammad.

Muhammad called upon the Lord and was visited by the angel Gabriel, who guided him to establish a moral system of government in the nation of the peoples God gave him to guide and care for.

3. By the time Muhammad finished his earthly mission, this growing nation included most of the Arabian peninsula in the Middle East. The Arab nations of today point to Father Abraham as their common ancestor. "Abraham" literally means "the father of the multitude." In many cases they have made the guide lines laid down by Muhammad into national laws.

4. **Muhammadans** as they are often called, consider Mecca, their prophet's birthplace, as sacred. Their favored religious symbol is the moon and star. The crescent moon symbolizes the controlled waning of evil-mindedness. The star represents the qualities of peace and light which arise when God's Love fills the mind.

Their Holy Book is the **Koran**. The word "Kara'a" means "read" in Arabic. Their churches have one or two **pairs of matching prayer towers** and are called mosques. They call the god of Abraham by the name "Allah" from "al-ilah", the God. They recognize Jesus, Moses and Muhammad as prophets of the Lord, but like the Jewish nation, believe that worship should be restricted to God in the formless state. They call their religion by the name "Islam", which means submission or surrender to the Will of God.

5. THE JEWISH RELIGION

The word Judaism refers to "those people who inhabited Judea in ancient Palestine". The Old Testament is their principal Holy Book. They are also sometimes called semite. This word means "the descendants of Shem", the son of Noah. Noah was the main character in the Biblical Flood Epic.

6. The descendants of Shem include the Arabs, Phoenicians and Assyrians, as well as Jews. Among them were the prophets Abraham, Moses, Muhammad and Jesus Christ. Thus we can see that the Jewish, Christian and Muhammadan religions spring from a common origin. This explains the many similarities.

7. The Jewish religion was codified by Moses the Biblical prophet, who received the ten original commandments from God. Judaism might more aptly be called Mosaic Law. When Jesus was born among this people He was variously received as a prophet, a religious trouble maker or a Messiah. Thus a split came about in the Jewish faith.

Some followed Jesus and Moses, others followed only Moses. Later many non-Jews began to follow Jesus and became known as Christians.

8. CHRISTIANITY

The followers of **Jesus** and the descendants of the Biblical Noah, Shem, and David, who follow Jesus are collectively called **Christians**. "Christian" means "followers of Christ". The word **Christ** means He who is filled with the Holy Ghost, God or Spiritual Light.

9. Jesus was born in the village of Bethlehem in the country of Palestine about 2000 years ago. Early in His life, Jesus began His search for God. During His worship of the formless God, he travelled through Iran, Russia, Kashmir, Tibet and India. At the age of 25, He realized that He was the Christ, annointed by God the Father to shepherd the people of Earth.

10. He returned to His native Palestine and after preaching there and performing many miracles, He was crucified in Jerusalem and His body buried. After three days of being One with the formless Father, He returned to the corpse and it revitalized. He then resumed His preaching mission. Later He returned to Kashmir where He left this earthly life. According to some sources, records of His life can be found in Tibet, Kashmir and India, as well as the New Testament.

11. Jesus upheld the Laws of Moses and sought to emphasise two more fundamental teachings. "I am in My Father, you are in me and I am in you." Jn. 14:20; and "Love your neighbour as yourself." Mat. 22:39.

His message is presented according to Indian sources, as: "**All life is One, my blessed Son. Be alike to everyone.**" This is also the basis of the **Eastern religion**, Sanathana Dharma.

12. ZOROASTER:
More than eight thousand years ago a people who spoke a language similar to ancient Indian Sanskrit travelled to Persia and founded a sister religion to Hinduism. The principal spokesman of their religion was named Zoroaster.

Zoroaster worshipped the One Wise Lord who created Life, Heaven, Earth and all of existence. His symbol for the formless, infinite God is the eternal fire of Truth, Wisdom and Divine Light. **Earthly fire** is used to remind the devout of the eternal brightness of the Lord shining within each of us.

Zoroaster taught man to live in harmony with the Creator, to avoid violence and follow the dictates of Divine Love. We see these philosophies emerge again in Judaism, Christianity and the Islamic religions which arose much later near the Middle Eastern home of Zoroaster. This religion formed a historic framework for the connection between the semite religions and Hinduism.

13. HINDUISM
Just as the Jewish religion is more properly called Mosaic Law, what is commonly referred to today as "Hinduism" is traditionally called "Sanathana Dharma". Hinduism has come to mean "the customs of the people east of the Indus". In Sanskrit Hindu literally means "restraint of the senses".

14. Sanathana means "timeless" or "eternal". The word Dharma means "Divine Law". Thus Hinduism is the religion of the followers of God's Eternal Truth.

Consider John's statement in Jn. 1:1 "In the beginning was the Word, and the Word was with God, and the Word was God." Does the "Word" differ from "Eternal Truth", Sanathana Dharma?

15. Like Judaism, Islam and Christianity, Hinduism is a monotheistic religion. Its followers recognize one God, who is the creator of all. He is called "Parama", supreme; "Atma", formless God.

The religion is represented by the Sanskrit word "om, 3". The "om" when pronounced produces a vibration similar to that upon which all creation is based. Just as ice arises and disappears in water, the entirety of creation arises from and merges into "OM".

Just as the Biblical celestial hierarchy includes nine levels or orders of angels and archangels, with varying numbers of wings and specific duties to carry out under God's reign, Indian Scripture descibes God not only as being formless, but as including various more or less angel-like deities. These are each responsible for carrying out God's holy orders in their own assigned areas on Earth and in the Heavens.

16. **Brahma** is assigned the role of God the Creator. He brings all new things into existence.

    Vishnu is God the Heavenly Preserver. Vishnu maintains divine harmony in the heavens and on earth.

    Shiva is God the Destroyer and Liberator. Shiva eliminates that which is hindering the evolution of Goodness.

17. Just as archangels are sometimes said to have six wings as a symbol of their high rank, Brahma, Vishnu and Shiva are often depicted as each having four arms. The upper pair of arms symbolizes their duties in the Heavens. The lower pair represents their role in earthly life. Some contemporary Christian and non-Christian religious groups pay varying degrees of homage to Jesus, Mother Mary, Moses, Abraham, or various Saints. Similarly different Indian religious sects concentrate on Vishnu, Shiva or Ganesha as their favored aspect of God.

18. **GANESH**
There is a Scriptural story that relates the following. Shiva, the Divine Liberator from sin, was given a son of Divine origin.

    Due to a trick of fate, He was assigned the job of heavenly gatekeeper before He had seen His father's appearence. He was told to let no one enter during certain ceremonies. Shiva attempted to go in. A terrific battle ensued. Shiva beheaded His son. Because His Son had done His duty well, despite His ignorance about His Father, Shiva replaced His Son's missing head. His new head was that of an elephant which had also been beheaded.

    He was then given command of the "Janas," Shiva's godly army. "Esha" means "commander". Thus He is called "Ganesha". In India today worshippers pay homage to Ganesha as the Divine Resolver of problems, the one who will meet any challenger which comes in the way of duty.

19. **Vasishsta** (Va-sish-ta) According to Indian tradition, during Earth's long history countless humans have attempted to know God and merge into His Divine Essence. Vasishta and Vishwamitra like Jesus made the struggle and found success in India.

    Vishwamitra (Vish-wa-mi-tra) began his spiritual conquest as a worldly king intent on worldly conquest. One day while travelling about, he became the guest of sage Vasishta.

20. During his meal he offered to buy Vasishta's favourite cow. When Vasishta refused to part with his beloved spiritual pet, Vishwamitra became enraged and attempted to seize the cow by force.

    At Vasishta's request God performed many miracles of deliverance.

    Vishwamitra became more and more obsessed with his campaign against Vasishta. Finally he realized that God could not be conquered by force. With this understanding Vishwamitra began to adopt the life style necessary to win God's Love.

    After many years and many set backs he eventually overcame his ill temper and won God's Grace.

21.   Later Vishwamitra acted as teacher and spiritual guide for King Harischandra. King Hari may be compared to David of the Old Testament. He was known for his virtue and regard for the duties God gave him. Like David, King Harischandra underwent many trials which added to his fame and place in history.

22.   His trials came at the hand of Sage Vishwamitra who tested him sorely and severely. The result was like the result of biblical King David's tribulations. King Hari gained the respect and trust not only of God, but of all of his people. He is remembered today for his adherence to Truth and Duty.

Another interesting parallel between King David and King Hari springs to light when we consider that God placed Lord Jesus in the House of David and Lord Rama, The Avatar of India, into King Hari's royal line.

23.   **Avatar** is a word of very ancient origin which is a combination of two shorter words; "ava" which means "down" and "tar" which means "to pass from above".

The word Avatar is used to mean God has come from above to the Earth plane. The Avatar comes to preserve or restore Divine Harmony on Earth and save mankind from destruction.

24.   According to Eastern tradition, the God who gave Christ Jesus to the West for its salvation, has come to India a number of times in the past.

Indian records tell us that God has taken a form appropriate to the needs of the people of each world age, in order to cultivate virtue and destroy evil. The lives of ten major Avatars are recorded in the Indian Scriptures. The first of the avatars came at a time when all the dry land on the Earth was covered by a tremendous flood. Just as God had sent the flood, He himself appeared to guide a boat, which contained representatives of all the animal species and a group of God-fearing men. Whether this is a description of the Biblical Noah's Ark, which is said to rest in a glacier on Mount Ararat in present day Turkey or of some similar epic, only God can tell us.

25.   The third and fourth Avatar maintained earthly harmony by destroying the **Gold brothers** whose Sanskrit names were Hiranyakashipu, which means "golden throne", and Hiranyaksha, which means "golden eye."

These two demonic Gold brothers, after many years of occult studies and power-grabbing schemes, gained control of the elements of nature and like Lucifer, in the Old Testament cosmology, had to be expelled.

26.   According to Indian Scripture, God as the Preserver of Divine Harmony came to earth in an awesome, superhuman form. This, the third Avatar, met Hiranyaksha's challenge, and after a great battle killed him and stopped his oppression of the good peoples of the world.

27.   Later Hiranyaksha's elder brother Hiranyakashipu sought to avenge his death. Hiranyakashipu first searched for God in the Underworld, which he then conquered. He extended his search for God into the Earth regions and after finding no evidence of God there, he became ruler of Earth. Next, with the use of his occult powers, he declared war on the Heavens and eventually became master of the spiritual beings who lived there. From his vantage point he attempted to stop all worship of God. He replaced it with worship of himself as the single ruler of the Underworld, the Earth and the Heavens.

28.   Needless to say, this began to upset the divine harmony of life. To bring things into balance and save the people of the world from unholy domination, God, as the Preserver of Harmony, sent a very high Soul to Earth as Hiranyakahipu's son, the divine Pralad, who worshipped God as the sustaining force of the Universe. As a young man who was the sole heir to the throne Hiranyakashipu occupied, he attracted much of his father's attention.

Hiranyakashipu insisted that he himself deserved all praise for the maintenance of creation.

29.   One day Hiranyakashipu challenged Pralad to show him this God He believed in so fully. At that point God took form as the fourth Avatar and destroyed Hiranyakashipu body.

Divine order was restored on Earth and in the heavens. After God himself ruled for a time, the faithful Pralad was given control of all that had form, second only to God.

These epics may, like the events related in the **Bible,** be taken literally as history or as stories to relay moral truths that help guide man on his pilgrimage to God.

30.   The seventh of the Avatars was named **Rama,** which means "God in human form". He existed on earth twenty thousand years ago. Like His ancestor King Harischandra, He was heir to the royal throne in India, which was then a vassal state of what the Greeks called Atlantis. Ravana, the ruler of Atlantis, had his capital on a now non-existent island near the Equator, in what is now The Indian Ocean.

Ravana, a very wicked King, commanded an army of friends and rogues, who delighted in committing atrocities.

31.   Rama gathered a volunteer army which included His most loyal follower, Hanuman. After a series of miracles which included the construction of a land bridge that connected the tip of the Indian peninsula and the Atlantean capital, a tremendous battle ensued.

Hanuman, single-handed, defeated each of Ravana's corrupt royal family. Rama personally dispatched Ravana into the next world.

Peace reigned on Earth under Rama's loving hand. Hanuman became an example of unwavering courage and devotion to those who know his story.

32.   Fifteen thousand years after Rama' a reign, the Krishna Avatar was born in India. Krishna existed in human form for about 185 years, after which He converted His body into Light. He, like Rama, was known for His captivating appearence. His hair style and facial features resembled those of the Sai Avatar of today. He was approximately five feet tall.

33.   During his mission on earth, He defeated numerous devil-worshippers who were taxing those who were leading virtuous lives. Thirty six years before He passed on, a tremendous battle broke out between the Pandavas, (the white brothers) and the Kauravas (the family) who represented the forces of good and evil.

Evil was overcome. Good prevailed and the Earth was cleansed and made ready for this current world age. The stories of the lives of Rama and Krishna are recorded in the two Indian Scriptures, The Ramayana, Rama's story; and the Mahabharatha, the story of the highest Truth.

34. At one point in His life, the Krishna Avatar gave religious counsel to a human He described as "the best of men". This conversation was recorded by sage Vyasa and is available today in book form as the "Bhagavad Geeta". Among religious literature the Bhagavad Geeta is second only to the **Bible** in the number of copies in print. Krishna's advice is just as applicable today as it was 5000 years ago.

35. The current Avatar has come to help mankind live in accordance with Krishna's advice and thus save humanity from self-annihilation.

Indian scriptural prediction bears a striking similarity to chapter 19 of Revelation. The tenth Avatar is described as appearing in the heavens riding a white horse. The Avatar is clad in a blood-red robe. He bears the name "Truth" — "Sathya", in the Indian Scriptural language Sanskrit. He comes for the salvation of mankind, as a servant of mankind, at a time when those in authority have grown corrupt. He is followed by legions of the righteous, clothed in pure white and He will bring peace, security and joy to the good people on Earth.

36. Indian scripture is very explicit about the birth marks an Avatar bears on His body. All of the necessary signs appear on the form of **Sathya Sai Baba,** who lives in South India today. Over thirty million people have acknowledged Him as the tenth Avatar. Ony time will reveal the accuracy of the full prophecy contained in the nineteenth chapter of Revelation and other world Scriptures.

37. Whereas Christians look to the Old and New Testaments, followers of Eastern spiritual science have numerous Scriptures to draw comfort from. The oldest holy works are called the **Vedas.** There are four Vedas currently in general use. They describe natural medical technology, the ideals of family life, social law, statecraft and religious practice. They also lay down the basis for spiritual growth, the divine ascension of the Soul and awareness of God.

38. Vedic spiritual science describes a Christ-like figure called a "Karana Janima". In English "karana Janima" means a divine human who is born with a divine mission.

During the last two thousand years, three "Karana Janimas" have come to India. Their missions involved the founding of three different spiritual philosophies, each based on Vedic spiritual science. Each of the three philosophies describes one of the three stages one must pass through along the road to **Christ Consciousness.**

Jesus in fact demonstrated and exemplified all three of these stages during His short life on Earth.

39. The Vedic spiritual philosophy, which describes the evolutionary stages Jesus passed through during the early part of His life, is called **Dualism.** It was founded by Madhavacharya, who was born in 1232 AD. He taught that all men are **God's servants** or messengers, and must carry out the duty God gives them, if they are to be happy and constructive human beings.

40. The spiritual philosophy, which embraces the Truth Jesus revealed when he announced "I am the **Son of God**" popularized in India by Ramayacharaya, is called **"Special Non-Dualism"** and is based on the Vedic statement "we are all God's children." As such, humans are encouraged to devote themselves fully to the love of God.

40. In the 9th. Century AD. Adi Shankara appeared in India. His mission required Him to establish a Vedic philosophy known in the West as **Non-Dualism.** Non-Dualism describes life when it is viewed from the standpoint of a Being who experiences Himself as being identical with God. Jesus declared Himself to be in the Non-dualistic state when He said, "**I and My Father are One.**" Adi Shankara's work revitalized the Vedic religion and helped men view all life as one whole.

41. Jesus had a very important role to play. He had to teach all three of the spiritual sciences necessary to progress from the ordinary human state to the state of full Unity with God. He did this staggering feat in the three brief years He taught in Palestine.

Today's Christians are indeed fortunate that a divine Being of Jesus' brilliance came to Earth to light the way, that we all might follow Him and join Him in full Unity with God.

Bibliographic Notes

The first four chapters of the Sai Christmas Book are Western English translations taken directly from Bhagavan Sri Sathya Sai Baba's spoken Telegu. Sound recordings were made of the 1976 1979 Sai Christmas Discourses which were delivered in India to largely Telegu speaking audiences.

The translated discourses are not in chronological order. They are arranged in sequence with the simplest coming first. The third chapter is an extraction of a discussion which took place on December twenty fourth 1978. Lord Sai kindly permitted His words to be recorded while He spoke with several Western pilgrims. Most of His Words were spoken in English. No translator was necessary.

The fourth section of the book is what may be called the application section. It is a synthesis of a number of questions which are relevant to the application of Jesus' teachings. Lord Sai spoke in Telegu and Sanskrit with some English terms interlaced as is usual for Him.

Some of the material in the sixth section also appears in other forms in the book "Sadhana — the Inward Path". Jesus' original teachings on traditional forms of prayer and worship have in most cases been lost over the years. It is hoped that this book will help to fill any gap in our current Christmas Scriptures.

GLOSSARY

Devil	see temptation
devotees	see disciples
devotion	see also faith, love. 1978: 134-6, 178, FJ: 53. G: 16.
Dharma	see also Divine Law, spiritual paths; G: 11-13.
diamonds	1979: 146. 1977: 153-4. 1978: 56-7.
difficulties in life	see also troubles. 1976: 14. 1978: 2-3, 57. FJ: 102, 129.
disciples	see also Judas 1979: 54-60; 1977: 84-90 1978: 801 W: 1-4 FJ: 33
discipline self	see self control
Divine Law	B: 10, 1979: 12, 21-34, 38, 55, 99-101, 104-28, 1976: 17-8, 88, 1977: 17-8, 21, 28, 31-2, 64-5, 109, 152, 156, 163-5, 172, 176-7. 1978: 105 FJ: 25, 32. G: 3, 13.
doors double	1976: 83
doubt	B: 9, 13. 1976: 44, 1977: 111 1978: 144 W: 1, 3
Dualism	1979: 40-42, 1976: 35-7, 57, 64-5, 67-8, 77. 1977: 87, 98, 106, 123. 1978: 12-3, 23-8, 36, 39-43, 123, 179-81, FJ: 27, G: 38.
duty	G: 20-1, 38.
Dwaita	see Dualism and Non-Dualism, Special
Divine Incarnation	see Avatars

E

education true	see also Truth B: 11, 16 1979: 1, 2. 1976: 74, 88-92 1977: 49 W: 5, 11
education worldly	1979: 1, 2 1976: 19, 21, 54, 74, 88-91 1977: 3, 42, 49. 1978: 50-54, 76. W: 6-9. FJ: 78.
ego	see also Bad, consciousness emotions, good, mind, self true, Soul. 1976: 20, 27, 83-7, 102. 1977: 31-41 1978: 50, 100, 1978: 131-3, 154-76, W: 27 FJ: 35, 63, 73, 88, 132.
emotions	see also anger, hatred, pride etc. 1979: 27, 179. 1977: 14, 1978: 131-3.
enemies	FJ: 64
English language	T, BN.
evil	See also Bad. 1979: 47, 88-93 1976: 20, 1977: 82, 1978: 103, 154-9 W: 23 FJ: 66. G: 23, 32.

F

faith	B: 9, 13 1979: 55-8 1977: 174
family	B: 11 1976: 21 FJ: 74, 88
firefly	1978: 135
Flood epic	G: 5, 23.
flowers	1978: 140
food	1979: 125, 1976: 11, 53, 98, 100, 105-6, 1978: 101 FJ: 64, 98.
force	see also power 1979: 2 FJ: 102 G: 17.
forgiveness	W: 22 FJ: 39, 52.
freedom	1977: 80
frustration	see also ignorance, sorrow, trouble, worry. 1977: 80.

G

Gabriel	G: 2
Ganas	G: 17
Gandhi	see Mahatma Gandhi
Ganesha	1979: 1, 1978: 1 G: 16-17
glass	1978: 56-7
goal of life	1979: 14, 28-38, 40, 157, 220; 1976: 9-14, 17, 20, 22, 37, 39, 50-1, 56, 97, 107, 1977: 4), 82. 1978: 145-55, 195-7. W: 16, 20-1, 33. FJ: 3, 9, 13, 113, 134.
Goal of religion	see goal of life
God	P, B: 1-17; 1979: 22, 25, 30-4, 39-43, 45, 49-50, 76, 77, 102, 130, 157, 184, 229, 231, 249-251, 255-62; 1976: 1-2, 5, 8-9, 12, 14-16, 18, 22, 31, 36, 39-45, 49-51, 57-77, 80-84, 92-9, 105, 108-14. 1977: 5, 12, 15, 28, 31, 42-3, 47, 54-5, 60-2, 80-2, 98-107, 118, 121-7, 135-40, 142, 144, 146-7, 154, 156-7, 163, 172-4,; 1978: 1, 4-13, 17-47, 96, 105, 111, 123-4, 130, 133, 140-5, 154, 159, 178-84, 188-9, 195-6,; W: 9, 13-4, 16, 18, 20-1, 25-6; FJ: 3-55, 61, 65-71, 74-5, 83-4, 86-8. 96, 98, 101, 104, 109-13, 117-20, 123-34; G: 1-2, 4, 8-11, 13-41, T.
God realization	B: 13, 1976: 82, W: 9, 10, 26, 34-5, FJ: 13.
God's Law	see divine Law
gold	1977: 155, 161-2, 172, 175.
Gold brothers	see Hiranyakashipu, Hiranyaksha
Golden Age	B: 17
Good	see company good, Good and Bad, good qualities, people good, people types of, spiritual practice.
Good and Bad	see also Bad, Good; 1979: 2. 1977: 19, 54, 177. FJ: 76, 115, 121, G: 23, 25, 27, 32,
good company	see company, good
good people	see people, good
good qualities	see concentration, compassion, contentment, detachment, devotion, duty, faith, Good and Bad, happiness, harmlessness, humility, judgement good, love, obedience, patience, self-control, wisdom.
Grace of God	see also Love B: 11. 1979: 302, 1977: 61-2, 1978: 193, FJ: 15-18, 127, 129. G: 19. T.
greed	1979: 11-12, 20-22, 26, 61-72, 1976: 104. 1977: 92, 169. FJ: 35 74, 80, 88, G:18, 24-8
grief	see sorrow.

H

Hagar	see Abraham
Hanuman	1977: 121-6, G: 30
happiness	see also pleasure, detachment; 1979: 10-14, 27, 65, 102, 106, 114, 127-33, 289-92; 1976: 33, 1976: 48-50, 72, 75, 82, 87, 90-1. 1977 9. 13-19. 80. 1978: 10, 45, 96, 100, 102, 132. G: 34, 38.
Harischandra	1977: 158. G:20, 29
Hari King	see Harischandra

181

harmlessness	B:6 1978: 72. W:22 FJ:69
harmony	see also Divine Law B:10, 14. 1979: 12. 1976: 88 1977: 20-1 1978: 4, 147; FJ: 13, 22. G:22, 24-5, 27, 34.
hatred	1979: 314-15 1976: 20, 30, 93, 102. 1978: 77, 131. W: 27. FJ: 74, 80, 86.
health	see body
heart	see also consciousness, mind, self true, soul. 1976: 32, 42, 97, 110-1; 1978: 1, 11, 21, 33, 37, 131-3, 136, 156, W: 12-4. FJ: 34, 37, 59. 61-2, 74, 85.
heaven	G: 14-5, 17, 22, 24, 26, 28.
Hedge, David	1979: 165-82
Herod King	P
Himalayas	1977: 101, 146. 1978: 18
Hinduism	G:12-7
Hiranyakashipu	1979: 25. 298-300. 1977: 157. G: 24-8
Hiranyaksha	1979: 25, G: 24-6.
Hislop Dr.	C: 1-6
Holy Ghost	1976: 76. 1977: 82, 104, G:8
Holy Spirit	1979: 156-60, 261-65 1978: 1
horse and cart	see cart
humility	1976: 59 1978: 177-9 FJ: 13, 99.
hymns	1978: 107 W: 11 FJ: 99
hypocricy	1976: 96, 108. 1978: 130, 135, 184-5, W: 7

I

"I"	see consciousness, ego, mind, self true
ignorance	P, B:10 1976: 45, 49, 51, 74, 93. 1977: 49-51, 55-6, 63, 71, W: 16-7. FH: 2, 7, 19. G: 17
impermanence	1979: 103-27 1976: 18 1978: 173-4
incense	FJ: 43
India	1976: 64 1977: 84, 103, 121, 142-3, 158, 163, 1978: 163. G: 9-10, 17-8, 23, 29, 31, 37.
Indian philosophy	see Dualism, Non-Dualism, Scriptures, Non-Dualism, Special.
individual differences	1976: 21-33, 93, 1978: 11. W: 15-6
Indus	G: 12
inquiry	1979: 43. 1977: 16. 1978: 18-9. W: 32
Isaac	see Abraham
Ishmael	G: 1-2
Ishwara	1978: 102
Islam	see Muhammad

J

Japa	see prayer
jealousy	1979: 63, 299, 314-316 1976: 20, 83-7, 102, 1977: 11, 41, 117. 1978: 78, 100, 131-3. W: 27 FJ: 63, 87-8
Jehovah	1976: 1
Jerusalem	1979: 47-8 1877: 23-4 1978: 61-91 G:10

M

Madhvacharya	see Dualism
Mahabharatha	G: 32
Mahatma Gandhi	1977: 158
Mary	P. G: 16
matchstick	1977: 57-61
materialism	see also pleasure; B: 13; 1979: 268-86, 296-8; 1976: 11, 44, 51, 98. 1977:14. 1978: 147 FJ: 21, 24, 73, 128.
Maya	see impermanence, reality
meat eating	B: 3
Mecca	G: 4
meditation	see also spiritual practice; 1979: 14, 1978: 18-22 FJ: 56-66, 70, 112-23, 120
Messenger of God	see Dualism
mind	1979: 132-3, 150-3, 157; 1976: 32, 87, 103. 1977: 71, 79, 80, 119, 121, 124, 133, 160, 173, 304. W: 28, 30-1. FJ: 45, 60, 66, 73-4, 78, 81, 83-4, 97, 103-4, 109, 125, 131, 133.
miracles	C: 1-6, B: 4, 9, 13-14, G: 10, 19, 30
misery	see sorrow
money	see wealth
money-lenders	1979: 47-8, 1977: 23, 26. 1978: 65, 72
monotheism	G: 14
moon	1979: 95, 1977: 148-9, W: 18
Moses	G: 4, 6-7, 11-12, 16.
mosque	G: 4
mountains	see Himalayas
Muhammad	1979: 1, 55. 1978: 93. G: 1-4, 6.
Muhammadans	1976: 1, 1978: 1, 46-7 G: 4, 14

N

nationality	1976: 21 W: 15
Natural Law	see Divine Law
New Testament	see also Bible G: 10, 36
Noah	G: 5, 8, 23.
non-Dualism	see also Unity 1979: 1, 49, 189; 1976: 60, 63-4, 70-2, 76-7, 1977: 84-5, 102-3, 125-6, 142-3. 1978: 12-3, 38, 45. W: 26, 28, 49, 103. G: 40
Non-Dualism special	1979: 43-6, 228-33, 1976: 57, 64, 66-7, 69-71, 75, 77, 1977: 86-7, 100, 124. 1978: 12-3, 29-31, 37, 44, 182-3. W: 25, G: 39

O

Obedience	1978: 193
occult powers	G: 24, 26.
ocean	1979: 36 1976: 25-8, 31, 89-91
Old Testament	see also Bible G: 15, 20, 24, 36.
OM	W: 18

reality	see also Bad, Divine Law, Good, impermanence, troubles; 1979: 78-9, 83, 103-27, 161. 1976: 9, 12. 1977: 13-4, 43-9, 63-71, 80, 123-5, 143, 167, 174, 177-8 1978: 8, 11, 17-19, 33, 36. W: 22
religions	B: 10 1979: 1, 213-18; 1976: 13, 19, 96, 1977: 81, 83-4, 142-4, 147, 150-1, 163. 1978: 46, 48, 50, 93, 195 W: 13. FJ: 14. G: 6. 14
Revelation	G: 34-5
rivers	1979: 36-8. 1976: 89-91
rosary	FJ: 49

S

Sacrifices blood	1977: 23-4, 28-31 1978: 66-72
Sadhana	see spiritual practice
Sai Baba, Sri Sathya	C: 1-6, B: 1979: 1, 1977: 128. 1978: 102 G: 31, 34-5, T. BN.
Saints	G: 16
Samsara	see Bad, Divine Law, Good, happiness, impermanence, life, reality, sorrow, troubles.
Sanathana Dharma	G: 11-17
Sanskrit	G: 34, T.
Sathyam	see Truth
Saviors	see also Jesus Christ, Krishna, Pralad, Rama, Sai Baba. B: 8, 14 1979: 211 1976: 18, 80, 1977: 12, 15, 81, 83-90, 111, 117-8, 120, 127, 130, 152, 156, 159-60 1978: 4, 14, 49, 55, 57, 93, 140-5, 194. G: 21-41
scandal	FJ: 63, 82.
science	1979: 25-6 1976: 53 1978: 162-3
Scriptures	see also Bhagavad Geeta, Bhagavatha, Bible, Koran, Mahabharatha, New Testament, old Testament, Shastras, Vedas. B: 7, 10. 1976: 45-6, 48, 65, 76, 91, 94, 112,; FJ: 25, 31-3, 37, 45, 56, 85, 134,; G: 1, 11, 13-4, 17, 21, 23, 25, 28, 32-6, T.
seeds	1976: 2
self confidence	W: 9-10
self control	1979: 26-7, 127-33, FJ: 101-111, 115-6, 120-23, 130
selfishness	see also ego, greed, materialism. 1979: 47, 84-9, 226-28, 314-16. 1976: 20, 22-3, 38, 97, 103-4 1977: 31-2 1978: 15, 100. W: 22 FJ: 20, 128
selfless service	see unselfish service
self satisfaction:	see also happiness, peace of mind. W: 9-10
self, true	1979: 89-95, 156-59, 249-55. 1976: 23, 27-31, 48-9, 56, 59, 81, 101, 112, 1978: 10-1, 171. W: 25, 30-1. FJ: 5, 7, 20, 29, T.
Semites	G: 5-6
Servant of God	see Dualism
Shakti	see love, power.
Shankaracharya	see Non-Dualism
Shanti	see detachment, peace
Shastras	1979: 49
Shem	see Semites
Shiva	1979: 1 1976: 1 1978: 1 G: 15-17
sin	see bad
sleep	W: 28

unselfish service:	B: 3-4 1979: 314-6, 1976: 57, 59-60, 64, 77, 80, 97-8, 114. 1977: 7-8, 11, 96-7, 172-3, 1978: 15-6, 52, 59, 92-3, 107, 132, 182. W: 22, 25. FJ: 6, 10, 13, 27, 69-70, 76, 99, 90. 120, 125-6, 128, G: 34

V

Vashista	1979: 21 G: 18-9.
Vedas	1976: 46, 48. 1978: 1, 46, 47. G: 36-40
Vishnu	1979: 1. 1976: 1. G: 15-6.
Vishishta Advaita	see Non-Dualism, Special
Viswamitra	1979: 21-2, 1977: 158 G: 18-21
visualizations	W: 52-4, 56
Vyasa	G:33

W

waste	1979: 8, 9, 20, 154 1976: 38, 53. 1978: 137-8.
W-A-T-C-H	FJ: 7/6 85
wealth	see also materialism 1979: 3, 7, 10, 12, 15-27, 6405, 69-80, 286. 1977: 20-5, 42, 92-3, 111, 113, 129, 153-6 1978: 1, 173. FJ: 24, 38, 73.
wisdom	B: 10, 1979: 16-27, 76, 81-7, 94-5, 134-44; 1976: 5-10, 46-7, 53-4, 74, 88-92, 96; 1977: 21, 51, 54, 64. 1978: 128, 147: W 23, 27, 32-3. FJ: 2, 8-9, 19, 22, 63, 89, 100, 104, 114;
work	FJ: 100
worry	see also difficulties in life, sorrow, troubles; 1976: 47; 1977: 13, 18, 65, 71, 80 FJ: 37, 75, 117, 118, 129.
worship	see also spiritual practice. 1979: 42;1976: 1, 113. 1977: 82, 122-6, 132, 134, 138-9, 141-2 1978: 62, 109-10, 116-20, 128, 130. FJ: 38-68 G: 26

Y

Yoga	1979: 133; see also judgement, good.

KEY

B.N.	—	Bibliographic Notes
B.	—	Biography of Bhagavan Sri Sathya Sai Baba
C.	—	Cross
FJ	—	"Follow Jesus"
G	—	Glossary
P	—	Prelude
T	—	Translation Note
W	—	Westerners' Interview 1978